LOVE
PORTIONS

Also by YVONNE YOUNG TARR
10 *Minute Gourmet Cookbook*
101 *Desserts to Make You Famous*

LOVE PORTIONS

A Cookbook for Lovers

by YVONNE YOUNG TARR

with illustrations by the author

THE CITADEL PRESS

Secaucus, New Jersey

This book is dedicated to the men in my life—
Bill, Jon, Nick, Jerry, Rick,
Rob, Nick, Todd, Mike, Ryan,
Nick, Nat and Youngie.

First edition
Copyright ©1972 by Yvonne Young Tarr
All rights reserved
Published by Citadel Press, Inc.
A subsidiary of Lyle Stuart, Inc.
120 Enterprise Ave., Secaucus, N. J. 07094
In Canada: George J. McLeod Limited
73 Bathurst St., Toronto 2B, Ontario
Composition by Schilling & Nichols, Brooklyn, N. Y.
Manufactured in the United States of America by
Halliday Lithograph Corp., West Hanover, Mass.
Library of Congress catalog card number: 71-186395
ISBN 0-8065-0266-5

Contents

shavers ✓ (handwritten)

Double ✓ (handwritten)

Double ✓ (handwritten)

[handwritten margin note: watercress / minced scallions / for olives]

Introduction

Are you in love, or do you hope to be? Do you dream of romantic candlelight dinners, long lingering breakfasts in bed (his or yours), sexy snacks on mornings after? If you have absolutely set your heart on sharing your life with a lover, whether it be for an hour, a day, a week, a year or forever, then this book is for you, because this is the cookbook for lovers. Its sole purpose is to provide recipes for two that are easy to prepare, spectacular to look at and delicious to devour.

There are, in this wide world, those who prefer to eat and drink and sleep alone, who prefer bran flakes for breakfast and TV dinners when twilight slips quietly into evening. There are those to whom cooking for a beloved is servitude and erotic cooking is a scandalous idea. To those I say, "Pass this book by."

But to you who believe eating can be a sensuous experience, especially when it follows, precedes or takes place during the love-making ritual, to you I recommend and dedicate this book.

LOVE
PORTIONS

Afters

What is more wonderful than loving? Nothing perhaps, except those luxurious moments *after* when your
senses are awake and *you're* very nearly asleep. Then
perhaps the most sensuous experience of all is to sip
something icy or to nibble some exotic tidbit. Here are
ten after-love-making snacks designed to make him sit
up and take notice–again.

Frozen Assets

Looking for something different to munch on a warm summer's night? How about vanilla ice cream, frozen in a crunchy chocolate cup of its own? Tuck these treasures away in your freezer, then—after—lace them with a smooth, soothing cordial and—devour.

INGREDIENTS

> 1 box fluted cupcake liners (the foil ones are best)
>
> 1 1-ounce bag of semi-sweet chocolate bits
>
> 1 tablespoon butter
>
> 2 tablespoons milk
>
> 1 tablespoon cooking oil
>
> 1 quart vanilla ice cream
>
> ¼ cup chocolate, anisette, cherry or banana cordial

DIRECTIONS

Stack several cupcake liners together. Repeat until you have 4 stacks. Plate chocolate bits, butter and milk in the top of a double boiler. Melt over boiling water. Stir until smooth and liquid. Rub the 4 inside cupcake liners with cooking oil. Use a spoon to spread melted chocolate over inside surface of cupcake liners. Freeze. Repeat process is chocolate cups appear thin around the top edges. Freeze until very hard. Remove one chocolate cup from freezer and quickly but gently peel off cupcake papers. Return this chocolate cup to freezer and repeat process with remaining chocolate cups. Place 1 scoop (or more if you like) ice cream in each cup. Wrap in Saran wrap and freeze. To serve, top with cordial and serve immediately.

Cream Puffs

The sweetest thing in his life (next to you) may well be these delicate and delicious cream puffs.

INGREDIENTS

PÂTE À CHOUX *(puff pastry)*
½ cup water
¼ cup butter
½ cup plus 2 tablespoons all-purpose flour
3 eggs

DIRECTIONS

Boil the water and butter together over high heat. Pour in the flour all at one time, and stir rapidly with a wooden spoon until the dough leaves the sides of the pan and forms a ball. Take the pan from the heat and beat in the eggs, one at a time, beating well after each addition. Your arm may feel a bit tired, but don't fret. It's a terrific exercise for firming the pectoral muscles. Continue beating until the mixture is smooth and has a slight shine. Drop spoonfuls of *pâte á choux* onto a buttered cookie sheet. Bake for 15 minutes in an oven preheated to 425 degrees F. and then lower the heat to 375 degrees F. and bake until the puffs are light golden brown (approximately 15 to 18 minutes) or until the sides of the puffs feel rigid. Do not allow the puffs to become too brown. Remove from the oven and set aside to cool.

FILLING

Prepare vanilla or butterscotch pudding following directions on the package, or use defrosted frozen pudding. Cut a cap off the top of each puff, spoon in the cream, and replace the cap. Sift confectioners' sugar over the cream puffs and chill until needed.

Chocolate Éclairs

One of the most succulent somethings I can think of for "afters" is the creamy chocolate eclair. The smooth, cold filling, the delicate shell, the sensuous chocolate frosting combine to spell "more."

INGREDIENTS

PÂTE Á CHOUX *(puff pastry)*
- *½ cup water*
- *¼ cup butter*
- *½ cup plus 2 tablespoons all-purpose flour*
- *3 eggs*

DIRECTIONS

Boil the water and butter together over high heat. Pour in the flour all at one time, and stir rapidly with a wooden spoon until the dough leaves the sides of the pan and forms a ball. Take the pan from the heat and beat in the eggs, one at a time, beating well after each addition. Continue beating until the mixture is smooth and has a slight shine. Pipe the *pâte á choux* through a pastry tube (no nozzle) onto a buttered cookie sheet. If you have no pastry bag drop a tablespoon of pâte â choux onto the greased cookie sheet and press into a 3-inch by ½-inch shape. Continue until batter is used up. Bake for 15 minutes in an oven preheated to 425 degrees F. and then lower the heat to 375 degrees F. and bake until the éclairs are light golden brown (approximately 15 minutes), or until sides feel rigid. Do not allow éclairs to become too brown. Remove from the oven and set aside to cool.

FILLING

Prepare chocolate pudding mix according to directions on the package or use defrosted frozen chocolate pudding. Split the éclairs lengthwise, fill with chocolate pudding (at room temperature), spread with frosting and chill until needed.

FROSTING

Prepare packaged chocolate frosting according to directions on package. Spread over top of éclair.

Irish Whiskey Ice Cream

Here's an ice cream you can make at home in fifteen minutes— no more. It's lace with Irish whiskey and crunchy chocolate.

I'll bet he becomes addicted after just one bite. Better whip up a quart, since this treasure can be found only in your freezer.

18 INGREDIENTS

1 quart coffee ice cream (the best you can buy)
⅔ cup Irish whiskey (the best you can buy)
2 thin Hershey chocolate bars, frozen

DIRECTIONS

Soften ice cream *slightly*. Spoon it into a bowl. Retain container. Stir in whiskey. Chop frozen Hershey bars into ¼-inch squares. Stir into ice cream. Return ice cream to container. Re-freeze.

Honeydew Melon with Pineapple Ice

A delicate blend of colors and tastes. A cool, light, summer-bright snack. The perfect climax!

INGREDIENTS

1 ripe honeydew melon
1 pint pineapple sherbet or ice
4 tablespoons Curaçao or Cointreau
4 mint leaves (fresh and whole)

DIRECTIONS

Cut melon in half with knife. Scoop out seeds carefully. Fill with scoops of pineapple ice. Sprinkle with Cointreau or Curaçao. Top with mint leaves. Serve immediately.

Cantaloupe may be substituted if honeydew melons are scarce in your area. Also, lemon ice may be easier to find than pineapple—the taste is different but still very good.

Chocolate Fondue

Does he have a passion for chocolate? Serve him Chocolate Fondue. He'll soon have a passion for you.

INGREDIENTS

> 9 ounces Swiss milk chocolate with hazelnuts*
> ½ cup heavy cream
> 1 tablespoon honey
> 3 tablespoons kirsch (or cherry or orange liqueur)
> 1 cup 1-inch pieces of angel food cake
> ½ cup candied cherries
> 1 cup ripe strawberries
> 1 cup tangerine sections

DIRECTIONS

Use a large knife to chop the chocolate (especially the nuts) into small pieces. Place the chocolate, heavy cream and honey in a fondue pot or in a small chafing dish. Melt over low flame, stirring constantly. Stir in the kirsch and cook for a minute or two longer. Serve surrounded by small bowls of tidbits. Use fondue forks to spear bits of fruit, cake, etc. Dip them into the melted chocolate, and devour.

*If Swiss chocolate is not available use any fine milk chocolate with nuts.

Baked Bananas with Coconut Cream

20

Try this delectable "island" sweetmeat and score an instant success.

INGREDIENTS

4 bananas (not too ripe)
2 tablespoons butter
4 tablespoons honey
3 tablespoons rum
1 cup heavy cream
1 cup coconut, grated

DIRECTIONS

Peel bananas. Melt butter in Teflon pan. Brown bananas on all sides. Add honey and rum. Cook for 3 minutes over medium heat. Place bananas and syrup in ovenproof glass baking dish. Bake at 350 degrees F. for 15 minutes, turning the fruit occasionally. Meanwhile place heavy cream and coconut in another saucepan. Bring to a boil and immediately turn off flame. Allow to steep for five minutes. Hold cheesecloth over the mixing bowl and slowly pour the cream through it. Pour coconut into cheesecloth and squeeze out the remaining cream. Discard coconut. Place the baked bananas along with their syrup in two serving dishes. Spoon coconut cream over them. Serve hot or cold. (If any coconut cream is left over, chill it and use it cold over any fruit or stirred into rice to use with curry.)

Sautéed Pineapple in Cream

Hot pineapple and brandy and cherries and ice cream . . . delicious!

INGREDIENTS

    6 *rings of canned pineapple*
    4 *tablespoons butter*
    5 *tablespoons kirsch*
 ½ *cup heavy cream*
    1 *generous pinch of grated nutmeg*
    1 *heaping tablespoon sugar*
    6 *Maraschino cherries*
    2 *scoops vanilla ice cream*

DIRECTIONS

Light flame under blazer pan on chafing dish. Put butter in blazer pan. Melt. Add drained pineapple slices. Cook until lightly browned. Sprinkle with sugar. Pour kirsch over pineapple. Cook for two minutes. Pour cream into blazer pan. Stir. Heat and serve over ice cream.

Caribe Whirl

. . . Cool, intoxicating and oh so curiously refreshing!

INGREDIENTS

    2 *cups pineapple juice*
    1 *cup orange sherbet*
 ¼ *cup rum*
    2 *tablespoons Pernod*

DIRECTIONS

Place all ingredients in blender container, cover and whirl until smooth and frothy.

Hot Buttered Rum

22

What is smooth and warm and absolutely intoxicating? Hot Buttered Rum and you.

INGREDIENTS

  2 *thick slices orange*
10 *whole cloves*
  4 *teaspoons maple syrup*
  2 *sticks cinnamon*
  2 *pinches nutmeg*
  2 *jiggers golden rum*
    hot water
  2 *teaspoons butter*

DIRECTIONS

Fill 2 heavy china mugs with hot water. Stud 2 thick orange slices with the whole cloves. Discard hot water in the cups and fill each with one studded orange slice, 2 teaspoons maple syrup, 1 stick of cinnamon, a pinch of nutmeg and 1 jigger of golden rum. Fill each mug with boiling water. Add one teaspoon butter to each cup. Drink hot.

a rum drink

Morning Afters

So you're a marvelous lover, but what else can you do? Man does not live by bed alone! Sooner or later morning always comes and with it an appetite . . . for food. Now's the time to impress him with your other talents . . . like your super cooking, for instance.

These ten epicurean breakfasts are so simple to prepare that you can whip them up while he's inside singing in the shower.

Honey Yummies

Here's a near-Eastern favorite as warm and golden as the Greek sun. These little fried toasts topped with honey and pistachio nuts will say, "I love you—even at breakfast time."

INGREDIENTS

6 slices white bread
2 small eggs
2 tablespoons milk
½ cup bread crumbs
3 tablespoons butter
8 tablespoons honey
½ cup pistachio nuts, shelled

DIRECTIONS

Cut bread into rounds, using a cookie cutter or a large glass. Beat eggs and milk in a bowl. Melt butter in Teflon skillet. Dip bread rounds in the egg mixture and then in the bread crumbs. Fry over medium heat, turning once. Top with honey and chopped nuts. Serve immediately.

Creamy Peach Rolls

A peachy something to serve with a steaming cup of tea or coffee.

INGREDIENTS

1 8-oz. package refrigerated crescent rolls

2 tablespoons granulated sugar

½ teaspoon cinnamon

4 tablespoons cream cheese

6 tablespoons peach preserves

8 tablespoons chopped walnuts

DIRECTIONS

Preheat oven to 375 F. Spread crescent roll dough flat into 4 rectangles. Mix sugar and cinnamon. Sprinkle each rectangle with one teaspoon cinnamon-sugar mixture. Crumble one tablespoon cream cheese on each of the 4 pieces of dough, place one tablespoon peach preserves in the center. Sprinkle each with one tablespoon chopped walnuts and roll loosely. Brush the tops of each roll with ½ tablespoon peach preserves. Sprinkle with teaspoon of cinnamon-sugar mixture and top each with ½ tablespoon chopped walnuts. Place in greased baking pan and bake for 18 minutes. Serve warm.

Strawberries with Honey and Rum Cream

Thinking of having breakfast in bed? Here's a honey of a way to start off your day.

INGREDIENTS

1 quart fresh ripe strawberries

¾ cup heavy cream

1½ tablespoons honey

1 tablespoon rum

1 tablespoon slivered toasted almonds

DIRECTIONS

Wash and stem strawberries and place them on paper towels to drain. Whip the cream with the honey and fold in the rum. Place the strawberries in a glass or silver dish, top with the rum cream, sprinkle with almonds, and serve immediately.

Apple Pancake with Sausage

Serve this large pancake for two when he drops in for Sunday brunch.*

INGREDIENTS

¼ cup all-purpose flour
2 tablespoons granulated sugar
1 egg
2 teaspoons cooking oil (not olive oil)
½ cup light cream
4 Brown 'n' Serve sausages
1 apple
¼ teaspoon cinnamon
2 tablespoons butter

DIRECTIONS

Mix flour and sugar. Beat the egg with the cream and add the cooking oil. Add egg mixture to dry ingredients and mix well. When ready to serve melt 1 tablespoon butter in a skillet and pour in the batter. Cook until golden brown over medium heat. Do not turn pancake. Meanwhile cut sausages into ¼-inch slices and fry until brown. Drain on paper towels. Peel, core

*Batter is best when made several hours or a day in advance.

and slice apple into ¼-inch slices. Arrange apple slices attractively on uncooked top of pancake. Sprinkle with sugar and cinnamon. Top with sausage slices and dot with remainder of butter. Cook for 2 minutes under preheated broiler, taking care not to burn. Remove from flame, cut in half and serve hot.

Baked Beef Hash with Eggs

In absolutely no time at all you can put this beef hash up to bake and get back to your guest.

INGREDIENTS

2 cans Broadcast corn beef hash
1½ tablespoons butter
2 teaspoons Worcestershire sauce
1 teaspoon sage
1 tablespoon dried minced onion
4 eggs
catsup

DIRECTIONS

Preheat oven to 350 degrees F. Place butter in a Teflon cake pan (heart-shaped would be nice). Place pan in oven until butter is melted. Mix hash, Worcestershire sauce, sage and dried minced onion. Spoon hash around edges of pan leaving a 4-inch hole in the center. Break eggs into this hole. Bake on bottom shelf of the oven for 50 minutes. Loosen hash from edges of pan, place serving plate on top and turn pan upside down. Decorate top of hash with stripes of catsup.

Nutty Pineapple Bread

A tasty "something" to serve with coffee—at breakfast, brunch, lunch, or just to munch anytime.

INGREDIENTS

1 package Pillsbury nut bread mix

1 egg

½ cup Lucky Leaf pineapple pie filling
  (or ½ cup crushed pineapple without liquid)

¾ cup water

¼ teaspoon allspice

¼ teaspoon cinnamon

8 dried apricots, finely chopped

¼ cup walnuts, coarsely chopped

DIRECTIONS

Preheat oven to 350 degrees F. Combine egg, pineapple, water, and spices. Add nut bread mix and stir about 70 strokes. Stir in chopped apricots and nuts. Grease and flour loaf pan. Spoon mixture into pan. Bake for 50 to 60 minutes or until toothpick inserted in center comes out clean. Cool approximately 10 minutes and then remove from pan. Cool. Serve with butter or cream cheese.

Peaches 'n' Cream

Ultra-luxurious breakfast or cool and creamy addition to a special brunch is this delightful recipe for fresh peaches and whipped cream served in a cantaloupe "bowl."

INGREDIENTS

1 cantaloupe, very ripe

4 large peaches, very ripe

½ cup heavy cream

2 tablespoons granulated sugar

DIRECTIONS

Cut cantaloupe in half. Cut a thin slice from bottom of each half so it will not tip on the serving plate. Scoop out seeds. Drain upside-down on paper towels. Whip cream until it thickens slightly, add sugar and continue whipping until cream is quite thick. Refrigerate whipped cream and melon halves. Peel peaches, remove pits and slice. Fold whipped cream into peach slices. Place each melon half on a serving plate, fill with peaches and cream and serve immediately.

Sausage Pancakes

If your love is the hearty-breakfast type—one who needs more in the morning than a nibble on your shell-like ear—better whip up this robust treat. Serve with fresh apple slices if you like.

INGREDIENTS

10 Brown 'n' Serve precooked sausages

1 tablespoon butter

1 cup Bisquick

¾ cup milk

½ egg, well beaten

   butter

   maple syrup

DIRECTIONS

Cut sausages into ¼-inch slices. Melt butter in Teflon skillet. Fry sausage slices until brown on both sides. Drain on paper towels. Beat Bisquick, milk and egg until smooth. Drain excess fat from skillet. Fry pancakes until bubbles appear around the edges. Arrange the sausage slices on the uncooked top of each pancake. Turn. Fry until brown. Slather each cake with butter and keep warm in the oven until all cakes have been fried. Stack pancakes and serve with maple syrup.

Bacon and Cheese Popovers
(Makes 8)

These melt-in-your-mouth morsels make you look like an accomplished cook even if you consider frying an egg a culinary challenge.

INGREDIENTS

2 slices bacon, diced
1 cup flour
½ teaspoon salt
1 teaspoon dried minced onion
1 cup milk
1 large egg or 2 small ones
¼ cup Cheddar cheese, grated

DIRECTIONS

Preheat oven to 450 degrees F. Fry the bacon until it is crisp. Sift together the flour and the salt. Beat the eggs into the milk and add this mixture to the dry ingredients along with the minced onion and the grated cheese. *Beat well.* Grease an iron popover pan or a muffin pan generously with bacon grease. Heat the pan in the oven for 5 minutes. Pour the batter into the pans until the cups are half full. Bake at 450 degrees F. for 30 minutes then reduce the heat to 350 degrees F. and continue to bake for 10 minutes more or until the popovers are browned and crisp. Slit the popovers and butter them. Serve hot.

Hearty He-Man Hash Browns*

Is there a man anywhere who isn't putty in the hands of a super hash-brown potato maker?

INGREDIENTS

>   *2 large potatoes*
>   *1 medium-size onion*
> *¼ teaspoon salt*
>   *3 tablespoons cooking oil*

DIRECTIONS

Quickly grate the potatoes on a medium-size grater. As you grate potatoes drop them onto several thicknesses of paper toweling. Press the liquid from the potatoes and carefully spoon them off into a Teflon pan with 1½ tablespoons hot cooking oil. (The wet paper shreds easily so be sure you don't mix any in with the potatoes.) Grate onion and add, with its juice, to pan and stir gently. Pat potatoes flat and fry over medium heat until brown. Use a pancake turner or spatula to cut flat potato cake

*These re-heat terrifically. Fry as directed and bake immediately prior to serving.

into quarters. Carefully remove potato quarters from pan and place on a plate. Heat 1½ tablespoons oil in pan, turn quarters and return to pan. Fry until brown. Bake for 15 minutes in an oven preheated to 350 degrees F. Serve hot.

Romantic Repasts

Your breakfasts are fantastic, your tidbits are a dream. You've snacked your way into his heart, but now the moment of truth is at hand. . . . You're about to prepare your first "Little Romantic Candlelight Dinner."

Never fear, help is here in the form of four fantastic gourmet menus . . . Mexican, Italian, New Orleans and French. First course, entree, salad, dessert and even drink recipes are here given for the most utterly devastating romantic suppers *ever*.

Mexican Dinner

Menu

GUACAMOLE

CHICKEN MOLE

TORRID TABASCO SALAD

FRITO CHEESE LOAF

NATILLA

SANGRIA

Guacamole Avocado Dip*

Cool and hot and spicy and *so good* with Fritos or Taco Chips! You're sure to love this south-of-the-border taste treat.

*Avocado turns dark and unattractive if prepared too far in advance. Better fix this about 2 hours before serving time—spread the top with mayonnaise and refrigerate.

INGREDIENTS

> 1 avocado (the avocado should be fairly ripe. Better buy it
>   a day in advance of your dinner party. Ask your grocer to
>   help you pick one that will be ready to eat in 24 hours)
> 1 clove garlic, crushed
> 1 tablespoon finely chopped onion
> ½ small ripe tomato
> 6 drops Tabasco sauce
> 2 teaspoons lemon juice
>   salt and pepper to taste
> 1 tablespoon mayonnaise

DIRECTIONS

Mash avocado with a fork until it is fairly smooth. Crush garlic over avocado and discard pulp. Cut tomato in half and shake out seeds. Chop tomato and onion and add to the avocado along with the salt and pepper and Tabasco sauce. Place in serving dish and spread the top with mayonnaise. Refrigerate. To serve, stir in the mayonnaise and serve dip with corn chips.

Chicken Mole*

Who ever heard of eating chicken with chocolate sauce? Millions of people, that's who. This popular Mexican main course is based on a chocolate sauce that isn't at all sweet but is spicy-hot instead. The chocolate makes the sauce rich and thick and doesn't taste a bit like hot fudge sundaes. Better try it—you'll never believe it until you do.

*Pronounced *mo-lay*.

INGREDIENTS

1 2½ pound frying chicken, cut in parts

1 tablespoon cooking oil

1 tablespoon olive oil

⅓ cup blanched, slivered almonds

1 tablespoon peanut butter

1 tablespoon flour

3 packets MBT beef broth mix

2 cups water

1 cup canned tomatoes, drained

1 teaspoon vinegar

1 tablespoon chili powder

1 teaspoon garlic salt

½ teaspoon cinnamon

¼ teaspoon salt

⅛ teaspoon pepper

1 square unsweetened chocolate

½ cup chopped onion

DIRECTIONS

Fry chicken parts in the 2 tablespoons oil until the meat is golden brown. Remove chicken from pan and set aside. Saute the almonds and peanut butter in the oil remaining in the pan. Add the flour and stir until browned. Add the MBT mix, the water, the drained tomatoes, the vinegar and the spices and stir until smooth. Grate the chocolate and add it, with the onions, to the ingredients in the pan. Stir until the sauce boils, then lower heat and simmer, covered, for about 50 minutes, stirring occasionally. Sauce should be quite thick. Add the fried chicken and simmer for 10 minutes. Serve immediately with yellow rice.

Torrid Tabasco Salad Dressing

Serve this tangy dressing over lettuce leaves and sliced canned beets for an easy and authentic Mexican salad.

INGREDIENTS

*⅓ cup condensed Campbell's bisque of tomato soup
    (cream of tomato may be substitued)*
1 teaspoon salt
½ teaspoon onion flakes
½ teaspoon garlic salt
¼ teaspoon black pepper
½ teaspoon yellow mustard
½ teaspoon granulated sugar
½ teaspoon Tabasco sauce
¼ cup lemon juice
½ cup olive oil

DIRECTIONS

Combine ingredients, except vinegar and oil; mix thoroughly. Beat in vinegar and oil alternately, beginning with vinegar. Store in refrigerator. Shake before using.

Frito Cheese Loaf

38

Looking for an easy way to impress your man? Bake him a bread as fast as you can.

INGREDIENTS

3 cups extra-light pancake mix

2 tablespoons instant minced onion

2 teaspoons chili powder

1¼ cups milk

¼ cup Campbell's tomato bisque concentrate

1 egg

2 pinches baking powder

1 tablespoon cooking oil

4 tablespoons Parmesan cheese

2 tablespoons Campbell's tomato bisque concentrate

½ cup fritos

DIRECTIONS

Preheat oven to 350 degrees F. Grease a loaf pan. Mix all ingredients except 2 tablespoons tomato bisque concentrate, 2 tablespoons cheese and the Fritos. Stir for 2 minutes and then beat for 2 minutes. Spoon batter into loaf pan. Spread the top with 2 tablespoons tomato bisque concentrate and sprinkle with remaining 2 tablespoons cheese. Stand Fritos up in the batter with points sticking up. Bake for 50 minutes. Cool for 5 minutes and remove from the pan.

Natilla*

So far your Mexican meal has been hot and super-spicy! Now for dessert . . . a delicate cream to soothe those tender taste buds and put you in a sensuous mood.

INGREDIENTS

> ⅓ cup granulated sugar
> 1 tablespoon cornstarch
>   pinch or two of salt
> 1⅓ cups milk
> 3 eggs
> 2 teaspoons butter
> ⅓ teaspoon vanilla extract
>   cinnamon

DIRECTIONS

Combine the first three ingredients. Stir in ⅓ cup of the milk to make a smooth paste. Beat the eggs, add them to the paste and mix thoroughly. Scald the remaining 1 cup of milk in the top of a double boiler, but do not boil. Slowly stir the egg mixture into the hot milk. Place over boiling water and stir constantly with a wooden spoon until the custard thickens slightly and coats the spoon. Do not overcook or boil, or eggs will curdle. Stir in butter and vanilla extract. Pour into tall individual dishes and chill. Dust with cinnamon before serving. Serve cold.

*Pronounced *Nat-ee-ya.*

Sangria

Try this wine cooler to warm him up. Here's a wine drink with so much punch you may never get around to serving dinner. A favorite in Spain and Mexico, where it's served by the pitcher full, a custom highly recommended for intoxicating evenings.

INGREDIENTS

1 bottle cold claret
1½ cups cold pineapple juice
¼ cup bar syrup*
2 cups cold soda water
1 lime, sliced
1 lemon, sliced
1 orange, sliced
6 Maraschino cherries

DIRECTIONS

Pour claret, pineapple juice, bar syrup and soda water into a large pitcher. Slice lime, lemon, and orange and drop into the pitcher along with the cherries. Serve cold with ice.

Sangria

*BAR SYRUP: Boil ½ cup granulated sugar with ½ cup of water for five minutes. Do not burn.

Italian Dinner

Menu

HAM AND MELON
LASAGNE
ANTIPASTO SALAD
GARLIC BREAD
FLAMING FIGS NERO
CHIANTI

Ham and Melon

An admirable beginning to any meal, especially an Italian one, is a tasty plate of cold melon slices with ham.

INGREDIENTS

½ ripe melon in season
8 slices cold cooked ham*
freshly ground black pepper to taste

*Prosciutto is best but if this is not available paper-thin slices of boiled ham will do nicely.

DIRECTIONS

42

Peel ½ melon, remove seeds and cut into 10 thin slices. Arrange 5 slices melon on each plate. Top with 4 slices ham. Sprinkle with freshly ground black pepper. Serve cold.

Lasagne*

Cook this Italian treat an hour or a day before your sexy Continental dinner party. Serve with Italian bread (garlic bread if you dare) and a simple green salad. *Magnifico!*

INGREDIENTS

- ~~2½ cups cottage cheese~~ *3¾*
- 12 Ronzoni "curly edge" lasagne noodles *18*
- 1 tablespoon salt *1½*
- 1 tablespoon oil *1½*
- 2½ cups cottage cheese *3¾*
- 1 egg *2 small*
- ¼ teaspoon dried tarragon leaves *⅓*
- ¼ teaspoon salt *⅓*
- 1 pound ground chuck *1½*
- 1 small onion *1 med.*
- 4 Swift's ~~Brown 'n' Serve fully~~ cooked sausages *cooked Italian 6*
- 2 14-oz. jars Aunt Millie's sausage-flavored spaghetti sauce *4½ cups*
- ⅛ teaspoon powdered cloves *¼*
- ⅛ teaspoon powdered sage *¼*
- ⅛ teaspoon thyme leaves *¼*
- 3 tablespoons granulated sugar *4½*
- ¼ teaspoon instant coffee
- ¼ pound mozzarella cheese *⅓*
- (Swiss cheese may be substituted)

*This recipe will serve four persons. A Lasagne small enough for two would not have enough soft cheese in the center. Never fear, however, it makes absolutely fantastic leftovers.

DIRECTIONS

Set a large pot of water up to heat. (From 3 to 5 quarts—the larger the better.) When water is boiling add 1 tablespoon each of salt and oil. Slip noodles into the water and boil until tender. Add cold water to the noodles and lay them out to drain on paper toweling. Place cottage cheese in small bowl of your mixer. Beat for 4 minutes, stirring occasionally. Add 1 egg, the tarragon and ¼ teaspoon salt and beat again for 30 seconds. Reserve. Crumble chopped meat into a Teflon skillet. Brown over medium heat. Pour off excess fat. Peel and chop onion and add it with the thinly sliced sausage to the chopped meat. Cook for 2 minutes more, then add the spaghetti sauce, cloves, sage, thyme, sugar and instant coffee. Simmer for 5 minutes. Place ¼ cup of sauce in the bottom of a 9″ x 9″ x 2″ oven-proof glass dish. Cover with 3 lasagne noodles. Spread a layer of the cottage cheese mixture over this. Dot with small pieces of mozzarella cheese. Cover this with ½ cup spaghetti sauce (or a little more if necessary). Arrange successive layers in like manner, ending with a layer of noodles. Cover these with spaghetti sauce and dot with mozzarella cheese. Refrigerate until serving time. Remove from refrigerator and let stand at room temperature for ½ hour. Preheat oven to 350 degrees F. Place lasagne in oven and immediately lower heat to 325 degrees F. Bake for 25 to 30 minutes, or until center is hot. Serve immediately.

Antipasto Salad

All the goodies usually found in an Italian antipasto lend their *zip!* to this crunchy salad.

INGREDIENTS

44

½ small lettuce head
2 slices salami
2 slices Provolone cheese
½ green pepper
4 scallions
8 pitted olives
¼ cup pimento strips
¼ cup olive oil
3 tablespoons red wine vinegar
Salt and freshly ground pepper to taste

tossed salad

DIRECTIONS

Wash lettuce and drain on paper towels. Break lettuce in bite-sized pieces and place in salad bowl. Slice salami and cheese into ¼-inch strips. Wash green pepper, remove stems, seeds and white pith. Slice pepper into ¼-inch slices. Wash scallions and chop coarsely. Slice olives. Drain pimento. Arrange salami, cheese, green pepper, sliced olives and pimento strips attractively on top of salad. Sprinkle with chopped scallion, oil, vinegar, salt and pepper. Toss and serve.

Flaming Figs Nero

This sensuous sweet may well be the something that set Rome aflame. Warm brandy-spiked figs with cool whipped cream, a perfect aftermath for a perfect day.

INGREDIENTS

¾ cup heavy cream
2 teaspoons granulated sugar
6 figs preserved in sugar syrup
6 tablespoons brandy

DIRECTIONS

Whip cream with sugar. Refrigerate. Place blazer pan of chafing dish over medium flame. Add figs and 5 tablespoons syrup from jar. Warm brandy and pour over figs. Light the brandy and allow to burn until flame goes out. Serve figs warm with a little syrup. Top with cold whipped cream.

Garlic Bread

Serve it if you dare! Garlic bread is so super-delicious it's a shame to pass it up even when you're in love. Munch it together and neither of you will mind.

INGREDIENTS

½ loaf Italian or French bread
¼ pound butter, softened slightly
2 cloves garlic, (or ½ teaspoon garlic powder)
salt

DIRECTIONS

Preheat the oven to 350 degrees F. Cut the bread in 1-inch slices without cutting through the bottom crust. Place butter in a small bowl. Slightly crush the garlic over the butter, scrape the garlic press and add the pulp to the butter. Cream the butter once again. Spread all of the cut surfaces of the bread with the garlic butter and sprinkle with salt. Wrap the loaf in aluminum foil and bake for 10 minutes. Open the top of the aluminum foil, raise the oven temperature to 450 degrees F. and bake for 5 minutes more. Serve immediately!

New Orleans Dinner for Four

Menu

BLACK BEAN SOUP

JAMBALAYA WITH CORN BREAD DUMPLINGS

LETTUCE WEDGES WITH PIQUANT SAUCE

PECAN PIE

RED WINE

Black Bean with Brandy Soup

(Serves 4)

Company coming? Serve this New Orleans style dinner and you're sure to be remembered for a long, long while (if not forever). Spiked Black Bean Soup makes a *wow!* of a first course.

INGREDIENTS

- 1 can Campbell's black bean soup
- 1 can water
- ⅛ teaspoon nutmeg
- 1 hard-cooked egg
- 3 slices white bread
- ¼ teaspoon garlic powder
- 3 tablespoons butter
- ¼ cup brandy

DIRECTIONS

Place the canned soup in a saucepan with the can of water and the nutmeg. Blend until smooth. Shell and finely chop the hard-cooked egg. Discard the crusts from the bread and cut the slices into ½-inch squares. Melt the butter in a Teflon skillet. Stir in the garlic powder. Add the bread squares and sauté over medium flame until golden brown, stirring frequently. Heat the soup over medium flame. Meanwhile warm the brandy in a small saucepan and set aflame. When the flame goes out, stir the brandy into the soup. Serve hot, garnished with the chopped egg and the garlic croutons.

Jambalaya with Cornbread Dumplings

(Serves 4)

Hi Dumpling! Try this! It's easy and a real show-stopper.

New Orleans style Jambalaya traditionally features a mouth-watering combination of ham, sausage, shrimp and tomato. *This* recipe takes deliciousness one step further and tops the whole lovely simmering stew with feather-light cornbread dumplings.

48

INGREDIENTS

2 ¾-inch — 1 1-inch slice from a Hormel boneless fully cooked ham
2 med — 1 large onion
2 strips bacon
3 ea — 6 Swift's Brown 'n' Serve fully cooked sausages
2 med — 1 large green pepper
1 pt. YO Canned Tom. — 1 16-ounce can Redpack tomato wedges
2 cup YO Tom J — 1 16-ounce can Mott's Clamato juice
3 YO Tom Past — 2 heaping tablespoons Progresso tomato paste
3 — 2 tablespoons granulated sugar
1 tab. meat concentrate — 1 package MBT beef broth mix
3 4" — 6-inch stalk celery, washed and cut into 4 pieces
¼ — ⅛ teaspoon fennel seed
½ — ¼ teaspoon dried thyme leaves
2 small — 1 bay leaf
¼ — ⅛ teaspoon rosemary leaves
12 ounces — 1 7-ounce package Carnation frozen "kitchen ready" cocktail shrimp. Frozen oysters if desired
1 package Aunt Jemima corn bread mix
1 egg
½ cup milk

DIRECTIONS

Chop the bacon and sauté it in an attractive heavy pot over medium heat for 4 minutes. Meanwhile peel and chop the onion. Wash, core, seed and chop the green pepper. Cut the ham into 1-inch cubes. Add the chopped onion, green pepper, ham, and sausages to the bacon in the pan. Stir until the onion and sausages are lightly browned. Remove the sausages and slice them into $1/2$-inch pieces. Add the sliced sausages, the tomato wedges, the Clamato juice, the tomato paste, the sugar, the MBT, the celery and the spices. Simmer, covered, for 1 hour. Add the shrimp and boil rapidly for 2 minutes. Remove the celery pieces and discard them. Heat the oven to 425 degrees F. Mix the corn bread, the egg and the milk. Lower the flame under the jambalaya and drop spoonfuls of this mixture onto the surface. Remove the pan from the flame and place in oven for 15 minutes. Serve hot.

Lettuce Wedges with Piquant Sauce
(Serves 4)

Cool, crisp, green and delicious, and a beautiful way to get your vitamins.

INGREDIENTS

1 small head lettuce
$1/3$ cup orange juice
2 teaspoons lemon juice
1 tablespoon granulated sugar
$1/3$ cup mayonnaise
$1 1/2$ tablespoons chili sauce

DIRECTIONS

Wash $1/2$ head lettuce and cut it in half to form 2 lettuce wedges. Drain on paper towels. To make Piquant sauce, beat together orange juice, lemon juice, sugar, mayonnaise and chili sauce. To serve, top lettuce wedges with Piquant sauce. Serve cold.

pecan pie

New Orleans Pecan Pie

Pecan is a pie among pies and not at all difficult to make.

INGREDIENTS

PIE CRUST

     1 box Pillsbury pie crust mix
     4 tablespoons cold water
2½ tablespoons butter

FILLING

  2½ tablespoons granulated sugar
    2 cups corn syrup
    4 tablespoons all-purpose flour
    5 eggs
  ¾ teaspoon salt
1¼ teaspoons vanilla extract
    2 tablespoons melted butter
  ¾ cup chopped pecans

DIRECTIONS

PIE CRUST

Mix butter with water and add to pie crust mix. Continue according to directions on package.

FILLING

Place first 3 ingredients in a bowl and mix thoroughly. Beat the eggs and whip them into the corn syrup mixture. Add the salt, vanilla extract and melted butter and beat well. Sprinkle the chopped pecans over the top of the pie. Place in an oven that has been preheated to 375 degrees F. Immediately turn the heat to 350 degrees F. and bake for 40 to 45 minutes or until the center is set but not firm. Cool to room temperature. Chill. Serve with whipped cream or ice cream.

French Dinner

Menu

BRANDIED FRENCH ONION SOUP

STEAK AU POIVRE

ASPARAGUS VINAIGRETTE

CHEESE ROLLS

BE-MY-HONEY MOUSSE

RED WINE

Brandied French Onion Soup

To bring out the French in you ... Brandied French Onion Soup. The easiest and best ever!

INGREDIENTS

2 slices French or Italian bread
1 tablespoon olive oil
1 tablespoon butter
1½ clove garlic
1 slice bacon, finely chopped
1 medium sized onion, thinly sliced
2 tablespoons butter
1 tablespoon flour
1 10½-ounce can Campbell's beef consommé
½ cup water
3 tablespoons Napoleon brandy
6 tablespoons Swiss cheese, grated

DIRECTIONS

Cut 2 slices French or Italian bread ¾ inch wide. Heat olive oil and butter in skillet. Add crushed garlic. Sauté bread slices until golden brown on both sides. Place one slice bread in each soup bowl. Wipe pan with paper towel to remove any burned bread crumbs. Sauté finely chopped bacon in pan for 2 minutes. Add remaining butter and *thinly* sliced onion rings. Sauté over medium heat until onions are soft but not brown. Add flour and stir. Pour in consomme, water and brandy. Bring to a boil, stirring constantly for one minute. Divide the hot soup between the 2 soup bowls, sprinkle each with 3 tablespoons grated Swiss cheese. Serve immediately.

Steak au Poivre*

May be cooked ahead, sliced and then heated in the oven if necessary*. Then, at serving time, call him in to watch as you cleverly add the brandy to the pan and set it ablaze. (Stand back or you may singe your eyelashes.) A very impressive dinner for two.

steak au poivre with parsley

INGREDIENTS

1 good-sized rump steak
1 teaspoon coarsely ground black pepper
¼ teaspoon salt
2 tablespoons butter
2 tablespoons olive oil
¼ cup brandy
3 tablespoons heavy cream

DIRECTIONS

Heat butter and oil in a large skillet. Press the pepper and salt into both sides of the steak. Cook for about 5 minutes on each side for rare. *(If you are preparing steak in advance, cook

*If you have prepared meat in advance, heat 1 tablespoon butter in a frying pan, add the brandy, lower the flame and set the brandy ablaze. Add the cream, cook for 1 minute and pour over the sliced steak. Serve immediately.

for 2 minutes on each side then slice the steak and arrange it in an ovenproof glass serving plate. Pour off the juices prior to flaming.) Cook steak "as you like it." Warm the brandy and pour it over the steak, and set it aflame. When the brandy has burned out, add the cream and swirl it around over the flame for a minute or two. Place the steak on a warm platter, pour the brandy and cream over it and serve immediately.

Asparagus Vinaigrette*

This is a cool salad to serve with almost any meal. It's also the most savory appetizer I can think of—try it both ways.

INGREDIENTS

1 package frozen asparagus
1 hard-cooked egg white, finely chopped
½ cup olive oil
3 tablespoons wine vinegar
¼ teaspoon oregano
¼ teaspoon salt
¼ teaspoon black pepper
⅛ teaspoon paprika
8 strips pimento

DIRECTIONS

Cook asparagus according to directions on package. Chill. To make Vinaigrette Sauce: Chop egg white. Combine all in-

---

*Make the sauce when you have an extra moment and store it in your refrigerator. It'll keep for a week and is equally tasty served over tomatoes, cold cooked string beans, etc.

gredients (except asparagus and pimento) and shake well. Arrange asparagus and pimento attractively on plate. Top with Vinaigrette Sauce. Serve cold.

Cheese Rolls

Nice 'n' cheesey and easy are these flaky rolls that add a flourish to almost any meal. Reheat any leftovers for breakfast the next morning.

INGREDIENTS

1 package Pillsbury Quick Crescent Dinner rolls
8 1-inch cubes Cheddar cheese
2 tablespoons milk
10 tablespoons grated Cheddar cheese

DIRECTIONS

Place 1 cheese cube at the broad end of each crescent dough triangle. Roll up according to directions on package. Brush each with milk and roll in grated cheese. Bake for 8 to 10 minutes in an oven preheated to 375 degrees F. Serve hot.

Be-My-Honey Mousse*

The smoothest, most sublime sweet *ever!* Be his honey—serve Be-My-Honey Mousse.

INGREDIENTS

  ¼ *cup honey*
  2 *tablespoons water*
  ½ *tablespoon unflavored gelatin*
  2 *eggs*
  1 *cup heavy cream*
  ¼ *teaspoon almond extract*
  3 *tablespoons chocolate syrup*

DIRECTIONS

Heat the honey. Sprinkle the gelatin over 2 tablespoons water and allow to soften. Spoon the softened gelatin into the honey and stir until gelatin is completely dissolved. Beat the eggs and while beating pour the honey mixture over them. Cook over hot water until mixture thickens slightly. Do not overcook! Place in refrigerator for 20 minutes. Whip cream until thick and add almond extract. Gently fold cream into honey mixture. Place one tablespoon chocolate syrup in parfait glasses. Spoon Honey Mousse into glasses, top with a touch of chocolate syrup. Refrigerate.

*Prepare a day in advance of serving.

Dreamy Desserts

Do you believe in the old adage, "Capture his sweet tooth and the rest of his beautiful body may soon belong to you too?" No? Well, nevertheless it's true! Men have a definite weakness for delectable desserts and dessert-makers.

Visions of sweetmeats and sugar plums may not be all that are dancing in his head, but as my great grandma used to say, "After the ball is over, a little piece of cake is not so bad."

There follow eleven dessert recipes so divine neither of you will believe you made 'em yourself.

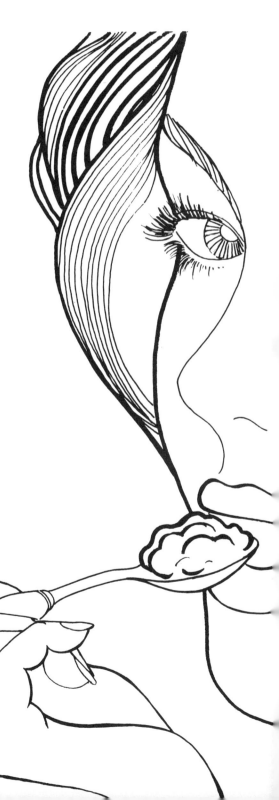

Brandied Strawberry Dessert Pancakes

... With your red lips redder still, kissed by strawberries ...

INGREDIENTS

BRANDIED STRAWBERRY SAUCE

- 1 cup fresh ripe strawberries
- 1 10-ounce package frozen sliced strawberries
- 2 teaspoons cornstarch
- ½ cup red currant jelly
- red food coloring
- ¼ cup brandy

DESSERT PANCAKES

- 1 cup orange juice
- ¼ cup milk
- 3 tablespoons cooking oil (not olive oil)
- 1 egg
- 3 tablespoons granulated sugar
- ½ teaspoon salt
- 1¼ cups all-purpose flour, sifted
- 2½ teaspoons acting baking powder
- butter
- confectioner's sugar

DIRECTIONS

BRANDIED STRAWBERRY SAUCE

Wash and stem fresh strawberries. Set aside. Place the package of sliced strawberries, the cornstarch and the jelly into electric blender. Cover and blend at high speed for about 1 minute. Cook, stirring constantly over low heat until thickened and clear. Stir in a drop or two of red food coloring. Add brandy and fresh strawberries. Keep warm over hot water until pancakes are ready.

DESSERT PANCAKES

Place orange juice, milk, cooking oil, egg, granulated sugar, salt, flour and baking powder in blender. Cover and blend at high speed for about 20 seconds or until smooth (stop blender once or twice and scrape down sides). Pour some of the batter onto a lightly greased crêpe pan or skillet and move rapidly back and forth and around to spread the batter thin. Cook until golden brown on one side and then turn. Cook until done but not brown. Spread with a little butter, sift with confectioner's sugar, roll up and keep warm. Serve several rolled pancakes on each plate topped with Brandied Strawberry Sauce.

Gingerbread Upside-Down Cake

If the trick is to treat him on Halloween, what could be sweeter than gingerbread masquerading as upside-down cake? Serve him this yummy cake with ice cream. Your rivals won't have a ghost of a chance!

INGREDIENTS

1 *package Betty Crocker gingerbread mix*
1 *cup lukewarm water*
1 *large apple*
2 *tablespoons soft butter*
2 *tablespoons molasses*
2 *tablespoons Domino Brownulated brown sugar*
  Vanilla ice cream

DIRECTIONS

Preheat oven to 350 degrees F. Grease sides and bottom of a square 9″ x 9″ x 2″ Teflon cake pan. Spread the extra butter evenly over the bottom of the pan. Mix the molasses and brown sugar in a cup. Spread this evenly over the bottom of the pan. Peel, core, and slice the apple. Arrange in a circular pattern over the molasses mixture. Place the gingerbread mix and 1 cup lukewarm water in the large bowl of your mixer. Beat 2 minutes at medium speed, or 300 strokes by hand. Scrape bowl often. Pour batter over apple slices and bake for 30 minutes. With a knife, loosen cake around sides of pan. Place serving plate over pan (hold it tightly!) and invert. Hold in this position for a few seconds. Remove pan. Cool slightly. Serve with vanilla ice cream.

Eve's Apple Delight

Some say apples make you lead a charmed life. That may or may not be true, but one thing you can count on is a warm reception to this crispy apple treat.

apple

INGREDIENTS

3 1⅛ oz. envelopes Instant Quaker oatmeal
(apple and cinnamon flavored)*
4 tablespoons butter
1 tablespoon flour
1 teaspoon baking powder
1 egg
⅓ cup granulated sugar
1 apple, peeled and very *thinly sliced*
1 tablespoon brown sugar
2 tablespoons chopped walnuts

DIRECTIONS

Preheat oven to 350 degrees F. Melt butter in one quart pan. Stir in oatmeal and flavorings, flour and baking powder. Beat in egg and granulated sugar. Butter and flour a 8½″ or 9″ Teflon cake pan. Spread oatmeal batter evenly over bottom of pan. Arrange apple slices attractively on top. Sprinkle with

*1¼ cup rolled oats plus ¼ teaspoon cinnamon may be substituted.

brown sugar and chopped nuts. Bake for 20 minutes at 350 degrees F., then raise heat to 500 degrees F. and bake 5 minutes more. Remove from oven and use a kitchen knife to loosen edges of cake. Cool in the pan for 5 minutes and then carefully loosen the bottom of the cake and slide it onto serving dish. Try it served "as is" with coffee or with ice cream for a delicious dessert.

Peach Melba

Ice cream topped with peach halves topped with raspberry sauce . . . easy and more delicious than you can imagine.

INGREDIENTS

2 scoops vanilla ice cream
2 canned clingstone peach halves
½ cup raspberry jam or jelly, strained

DIRECTIONS

Place 1 scoop of ice cream in each of two small glass dishes. Top with ½ drained peach half and ¼ cup strained raspberry jelly. Serve immediately.

Swedish Apple Spice Cake*
(Serves 8)

Here's a spice cake with a moist apple filling baked right inside. Just top with a dollop of whipped cream for a dandy company dessert.

---

*There are times when oven lovers must have company. For those moments try this company dessert.

INGREDIENTS

    1 box Duncan Hines spice cake mix
    1¼ cups canned sweetened apple pie filling
    ¼ teaspoon nutmeg
    ¼ teaspoon cinnamon
    1 cup heavy cream
    1 tablespoon granulated sugar

DIRECTIONS

Prepare spice cake mix according to directions on the package. Mix apple pie filling, nutmeg and cinnamon.

Place batter in a large greased tube pan. Drop spoonfuls of apple filling into the batter all around the cake. Bake for 65 minutes in an oven preheated to 350 degrees F. Cool cake in pan. Meanwhile whip heavy cream and sugar. Chill.

Use a knife to loosen cake around sides of pan and around center tube. Place serving plate over top of pan and invert. (If top of cake sticks to pan, gently loosen and arrange broken parts neatly on top of cake.) Top cake with whipped cream. Serve immediately.

Rose-Bowl Red Fruit

Heap champagne glasses with red fruits—watermelon, straw-

red fruit

berries and raspberries. Top with raspberry sauce and a little Kirsch . . . fantastic!

INGREDIENTS

1 cup frozen raspberries, thawed

2 tablespoons kirsch

1 cup watermelon balls

½ cup fresh raspberries

1 cup ripe strawberries

DIRECTIONS

Place thawed raspberries and syrup in container of blender. Blend for 1 minute. Strain, add the kirsch, and refrigerate the sauce. Cut melon balls, wash raspberries. Wash and stem strawberries. When ready to serve, heap fruit in champagne glasses or glass dishes, top with sauce and serve very cold.

Cherry and Pineapple Turnovers
(Makes 8)

If you know you'll be dropping back "to your place" after the movies and you'd like something hot 'n' sweet to munch either before or after the main feature, by all means try these. Make 'em in the morning and reheat later on.

INGREDIENTS

TURNOVERS

1 box Pillsbury pie crust mix

4 tablespoons cold water

4 tablespoons butter

1½ cups Crisco cooking oil

FRUIT FILLING

    ½ cup canned cherry pie filling
    ½ cup pineapple pie filling
    ⅛ teaspoon cinnamon
    2 tablespoons walnuts, chopped

DIRECTIONS

TURNOVERS

Combine melted butter with water. Use a fork to stir one package Pillsbury pie crust mix. Stir with a fork until dough holds together. Form into a ball. Sprinkle flour on pastry board or cloth. Rub flour on rolling pin. Roll out to ¼ inch thick and cut into 4-inch squares. Gently lift the squares, one at a time, and place 1 heaping tablespoon fruit filling on one side of the square. Wet the edges of the pastry, fold over and press together. Flute the edges with thumb and forefinger. Fry in hot oil and butter, turning once, until the pies are *brown* on each side. Serve immediately or make in the morning, place on a cookie sheet lined with aluminum foil, roll each pie in cinnamon and sugar, and reheat later for 20 minutes in an oven preheated to 325 degrees F. Do not refrigerate after frying.

FRUIT FILLING

Mix all ingredients together.

Chewy Chocolate Candy Cake*

The sexiest texture and taste ever in a cake! If he loves chocolate he'll adore you for making this!

*There are times when even lovers must have company. For those moments try this company dessert.

INGREDIENTS

30 *Kraft caramels*
1 *6-ounce bag Nestlés semi-sweet chocolate bits*
1 *tablespoon butter*
¼ *cup heavy cream*
1 *15.5-ounce box Betty Crocker fudge brownie mix*
2 *medium size eggs*
¼ *cup water*
1 *tablespoon heavy cream*
½ *roll of Pillsbury's Slice and Bake chocolate chip cookies*
¾ *cup heavy cream*
2 *teaspoons granulated sugar*

DIRECTIONS

Place caramels, chocolate bits, butter and ¼ cup heavy cream in the top of a double boiler. Stir over boiling water until caramels are melted and mixture is smooth. Cool to room temperature. Grease the bottom and sides of a glass or Teflon 8″ square dish or pan. Cut the cookie slices ¼ inch thick and press them into the bottom of the dish until it is completely covered. Mix Brownie mix, eggs and one tablespoon heavy cream. Spread ½ of batter over the cookie slices. Spread ½ of caramel mix over this. Cover with remaining batter and top this with remaining caramel mixture. Bake at 350 degrees F. for 40 minutes. Cool completely. Meanwhile whip ¾ cup heavy cream and sugar. Serve squares of the cake topped with cold whipped cream.

Russian Fruit Soup

If you've never heard of a dessert soup you're in for a very pleasant surprise. This is also a nice cool "soup break" on a hot Sunday afternoon.

INGREDIENTS

   1 *package frozen strawberries in syrup*

   2 *tablespoons sugar*

¼ *cup claret*

   4 *tablespoons water*

¼ *cup sour cream*

     pinch of nutmeg

     pinch of cloves

30 *strawberries (whole)*

DIRECTIONS

Blend frozen strawberries and sugar in blender. Pour into mixing bowl. Stir in sour cream. Add water and claret and stir until smooth. Wash and stem fresh berries. Serve soup in bowls garnished with 15 whole berries each.

(To serve hot, omit whole berries and slowly bring the soup to steaming. Do not boil.)

Almond Apricots*

Sometimes the simple desserts are the most welcome....This one practically prepares itself.

INGREDIENTS

½ *box fancy dried apricots*

   1 *cup canned apricot nectar*

¼ *cup granulated sugar*

   3 *tablespoons Cointreau or apricot brandy*

¾ *cup* whole blanched *almonds*

*Apricots must marinate in the juice for 2 days prior to serving.

DIRECTIONS

Wash the apricots and place them in a medium-size glass dish. Mix the apricot nectar, sugar and Cointreau and pour the liquid over the fruit. Place in the refrigerator for two days, stirring occasionally. To serve, stir in the almonds. Serve cold.

Strawberries Romanoff

For some reason strawberries seem to say "I love you." Perhaps it's because everyone loves *them* so much.

INGREDIENTS

1 quart ripe strawberries
⅓ cup granulated sugar
½ cup orange juice (freshly squeezed is best)
¼ cup Cointreau
¾ cup heavy cream
1½ tablespoons granulated sugar

DIRECTIONS

Wash the berries, discard the hulls, and drain thoroughly. Place the berries in a glass bowl. Squeeze and strain the orange juice, mix it with ⅓ cup sugar and the Cointreau and pour the liquid over the berries. Chill for 1 hour. Meanwhile beat the cream until it begins to thicken, sprinkle in 1½ tablespoons sugar and continue to beat until the cream is quite stiff. To serve use a pastry tube with a fluted nozzle to pipe points of whipped cream over the berries and liquid. Serve immediately.

Go-on-to-His-House

When you're sipping a drink in some secluded café and he whispers, "Let's slip back to my place and stir up something interesting," he may or may not have dinner on his mind.

Whether he's looking for a good meal or a good time—or both—it's a great idea to have a few super-simple dishes you can toss together with a minimum amount of shopping and preparation time.

If he offers to do the honors, cooking-wise, all the better. You take charge of the dessert and/or the "o-o-ohing and a-a-ahing."

Chicken Teriyaki

The flavor here is a little Oriental, more than a little South Sea island—*very* special.

INGREDIENTS

1 small frying chicken, cut into pieces
1 cup brown sugar
⅓ cup dark rum
½ cup soy sauce
1 clove garlic, crushed
1 green pepper
1 cup canned pineapple chunks
1 cup minute rice

DIRECTIONS

Wash and dry chicken parts. Mix brown sugar, rum, soy sauce and crushed garlic. Arrange chicken pieces in flat glass baking dish and pour brown sugar mixture over them. Marinate overnight, turning chicken pieces once. Approximately 1½ hours before serving time, wash green pepper, discard stem, seeds and white pulp and cut pepper into 1 inch squares. Drain pineapple chunks. Bake chicken ½ hour at 350 degrees F., then turn chicken, green pepper pieces and pineapple chunks, and bake 30 minutes more. Serve hot on a bed of rice.

Batter-Fried Chicken*

Strictly southern style and crispy as can be. Serve it hot with fruit sauce for a meal that's fast and fantastic.

INGREDIENTS

1 2½ pound frying chicken, cut in pieces
2 tablespoons cooking oil
1 cup flour
1½ cups beer
1 egg
½ teaspoon salt
½ teaspoon thyme
cooking oil for deep frying

DIRECTIONS

Pull skin from chicken pieces. Place 2 tablespoons oil in skillet. Cook over medium-low flame until chicken is done (about 20 minutes), turning once. Cool chicken to room temperature.

Beat together flour, beer, egg, salt and thyme. Heat oil in deep fryer or skillet. Place aluminum foil on a cookie sheet. Heat oven to 250 degrees F. Dip chicken in batter and fry one or two pieces at a time. Drain for a few seconds on paper toweling then place on cookie sheet in oven to keep warm until all chicken is fried. Sprinkle with salt. Serve at once with or without Hot Fruit Sauce (page 74).

*May be partially prepared one day in advance. Deep fry just before serving.

Foie Gras Spaghetti

Super sumptuous! Smooth and creamy Foie Gras sauce is the ultimate in sensuous eating. If you're skeptical, try it and see!

INGREDIENTS

1 chicken breast, boned and skinned
1 2¾-ounce can Hafner brand foie gras
3 tablespoons butter
2 tablespoons brandy
½ pint heavy cream
2 packets MBT chicken broth mix
8 ounces Ronzoni linguine 17 (flat spaghetti)
Salted water for cooking spaghetti
freshly ground pepper

DIRECTIONS

Cook spaghetti according to directions on package: Cut chicken into 1-inch cubes. Drain on paper towels. Melt butter in skillet. Cook chicken cubes for 2 minutes on each side. Add brandy, heat and set aflame. Add foie gras, heavy cream and MBT chicken broth mix. Mix well. Bring to a boil and continue to boil for 1 minute. Drain spaghetti thoroughly. Pour sauce over spaghetti, toss and serve immediately with freshly ground pepper to taste.

Caviar Omelette

Caviar for breakfast, lunch or dinner.... How posh! How luxurious! How loving!

INGREDIENTS

  4 eggs
  2 tablespoons milk
  2 tablespoons butter
  1½ tablespoons cream cheese
  2 ounces red caviar
    freshly ground black pepper

DIRECTIONS

Separate yolks and white of eggs. Beat the whites until they are *almost* stiff. Mix the milk with the yolks. Fold the whites into the egg yolk mixture. Melt the butter in a Teflon skillet. Pour in the eggs and cook over medium-low heat until the top begins to set. Dot with small bits of cream cheese and place under a broiler for a minute or two. Remove from broiler, top with caviar and carefully loosen and fold over the omelette. Turn onto a plate, cut in half, top with pepper, and serve immediately.

Cheese Fondue

There is nothing but *nothing* that goes better with beer than Cheese Fondue. Impressive too.

INGREDIENTS

  1 cup grated Swiss cheese
  ⅔ cup milk
  1 tablespoon butter
  ⅓ teaspoon dry mustard
  ½ cup fine bread crumbs
  1 egg, beaten slightly
    dash or two of cayenne pepper
  2 hard rolls

DIRECTIONS

Light Sterno under blazer pan of fondue or chafing dish. Melt butter. Add milk, dry mustard, grated cheese, bread crumbs and cayenne pepper. Stir constantly until cheese is melted. Leave on very low flame, while you cut the hard rolls into bite-sized pieces. Place bread pieces in bread basket. In measuring cup beat lightly the egg with a fork. Beat into cheese mixture. Serve immediately over low flame. Spear pieces of bread with a fork and dunk in cheese mixture. Eat—then spear again. Etc.

Hot Fruit Sauce

This ruby red fruit sauce is super when served with any pork or poultry dish, but it's really best with Batter Fried Chicken or Nutty but Nice Fried Shrimp.

INGREDIENTS

1 box frozen red raspberries, thawed
1 drop red food coloring
1 packet MBT beef broth mix
4 whole cloves
¼ teaspoon cinnamon
2 tablespoons rum
2 teaspoons cornstarch
2 tablespoons cold water

DIRECTIONS

Force thawed raspberries through a strainer and discard seeds. Mix raspberry juice, food coloring, beef broth mix, cloves, cinnamon and rum in a small saucepan. Bring to a boil. Mix cornstarch and cold water and stir into hot fruit juice mixture. Bring to a boil, stirring constantly until sauce is clear and thickened. Serve hot.

Nutty But Nice Fried Shrimp

Here's a dish that's fit for a king . . . or anyone who happens to be around at the moment.

INGREDIENTS

16 *large raw shrimp, shelled*
½ *cup flour*
¾ *cup beer*
½ *egg, beaten*
¼ *teaspoon salt*
¾ *cup chopped almonds*
    cooking oil for deep frying

DIRECTIONS

Remove shells from shrimp and make a fairly deep cut down the back of each. Do not cut through. Remove dark veins. Heat oil in deep fryer or skillet. Beat together flour, beer, egg and salt. Dip shrimp in batter and roll in chopped almonds. Deep fry a few at a time. Drain on paper towels and keep warm in oven until all shrimp are fried. Serve at once with Hot Fruit Sauce (page 74).

Oriental Oranges with Ambrosia Cream

"Ambrosia with an Oriental flavor"..."Food of the God of the East"..."A tidbit to soothe or stimulate"...or at any rate something quick to prepare and absolutely delicious to eat.

INGREDIENTS

2 10-ounce cans Mandarin orange sections, cold
4 tablespoons maple syrup
4 tablespoons sour cream (if sour cream is not to your liking, substitute whipped cream)
6 drops almond extract
generous sprinkling of nutmeg

DIRECTIONS

Drain Mandarin orange sections. Divide equally between 2 champagne glasses. Top each with 2 tablespoons maple syrup. Flavor cream with almond extract. Top orange sections with cream. Sprinkle with nutmeg. Serve cold.

Kahlua Parfait*

This parfait goes all the way on flavor. Try it!

INGREDIENTS

1 pint coffee ice cream
1 jar marrons glacé in vanilla syrup
¼ cup Kahlua
whipped cream

*A Kahlua sundae is equally delicious. Simple place ice cream in a dish, then top with marrons glacé and pour Kahlua over all.

parfait

DIRECTIONS

Place 1 tablespoon Kahlua in the bottom of each of 2 parfait glasses. Top with ice cream then marrons glacé with a little syrup. Repeat the layers (Kahlua, ice cream, marrons glacé) until the glass is filled. Top with whipped cream. Keep in freezer until needed.

Iced Coffee with Ice Cream and Brandy

If the game's in the hot last quarter and there's weather outside to match, perhaps you and the man in your life would welcome a glass of icy coffee and ice cream spiked with brandy.

INGREDIENTS

2 heaping teaspoons instant coffee
  cold water
2 scoops ice cream
4 tablespoons brandy
  sugar to taste

DIRECTIONS

Place 1 heaping teaspoon (or more if you like extra-strong iced coffee) instant coffee in each of two glasses. Fill ¾ full with cold water. Stir. Add 1 scoop of ice cream and 2 tablespoons brandy to each and stir once more. Sugar if desired. Serve immediately.

His Sporting Life

Are you a sporty couple? Do you spend most of your life together on the 50-yard line, or behind the batter's mound, or dodging hockey pucks?

Come June, do you only see the back of his head and the front of the TV set? Do you kiss during the commercials and make love when the home team is out of town? And, in spite of that, are you still really crazy about the guy?

There follows a bunch of recipes for lusty, gusty, fill-him-up-after-the-game eatables that'll make you an indispensable part of his sporting life.

Steak Sandwich

Here's a hearty, he-man TV snack! Steak topped with mushrooms and onions served on scooped-out Italian bread. Delicious!

INGREDIENTS

> 2 minute steaks
> 1 tablespoon cooking oil
> 1 tablespoon butter
> 1 large onion
> 4 large fresh mushrooms
> 1 small ripe tomato
> 1 packet MBT beef broth mix
> ⅛ teaspoon ground sage
> ⅛ teaspoon thyme leaves or powdered thyme
> 1 loaf Italian bread
>   salt and pepper
>   sprinkle of garlic if you both don't mind

DIRECTIONS

Place oil and butter in a Teflon frying pan. Stir over medium heat. Add steaks, brown on each side, cook to desired degree of doneness and set aside. Peel the onion and cut into ¼-inch slices. Wash the mushrooms, remove the stems and slice the caps into ¼-inch slices. Peel the tomato, shake out the seeds and chop. Separate the onion slices into rings and sauté them, with the mushroom slices, in the oil in the pan. Stir frequently. When the vegetables are browned slightly, add the chopped tomato, the MBT broth mix (*no* water) and the seasonings. Cook, stirring for 3 minutes. Add the steaks to reheat. Slice the Italian bread lengthwise and cut it in half. Pull some of the soft bread from the insides and place the cut loaf under the broiler (1 minute on each side). Spoon the cooked vetgetables into the hollow of the bottom halves of the bread. Place the steak on top of this, top with the remaining vegetables, and serve hot.

Franks for the Memories*

A terribly silly title, I'll admit, but one with a message. These franks, wrapped in cheese and flaky bisquit blankets, are TV snacks he'll remember long after the game is over.

INGREDIENTS

4 "American" Kosher frankfurters (or others)
4 strips Swift's bacon
½ 8-ounce package Pillsbury quick crescent dinner rolls
1 teaspoon Grey Poupon Dijon mustard
4 1-inch squares Kraft Velveeta cheese

DIRECTIONS

Peel the frankfurters and wrap one slice of bacon around the full length of each. Broil until bacon is rather crisp but not burned. Cool bacon-wrapped franks on paper toweling. Unroll the dough and separate 4 triangles. Spread with mustard. (Reserve remainder of dough for another time or prepare chili dogs for an interesting variety.) Cut the cheese cubes in half and place them, with the bacon-wrapped franks, on the crescent dough. Seal in the cheese by pressing the ends of the dough around the frank. Place on an ungreased cookie sheet and bake for 10 minutes in an oven preheated to 375 F. Serve hot.

*If you like, broil the franks in the morning and bake later.

Fried Meat Pies

(Makes 8 little pies)

82

These fab meat pies will open his eyes to what the right girl with the right recipe can do to enhance his sporting life. Cook in advance, then heat and serve with beer. Absolutely perfect!

INGREDIENTS

CRUST

1 box Pillsbury pie crust mix

4 tablespoons cold water

4 teaspoons butter

1½ cups Crisco cooking oil

BEEF AND SAUSAGE FILLING

4 Brown 'n' Serve sausages

½ pound lean ground beef

1 medium size onion, peeled and finely chopped

¼ teaspoon sage

shake or two or powdered cloves

1 envelope MBT beef broth mix

1 teaspoon Gravy Master

2 tablespoons catsup

HAM FILLING

1 slice bacon

1 cup chopped cooked ham

1 medium size onion, peeled and chopped

½ large tomato, peeled

1 teaspoon Grey Poupon mustard (or Mister Mustard)

2 tablespoons heavy cream or milk

DIRECTIONS

CRUST

Combine melted butter with water. Use a fork to stir this mixture into 1 package Pillsbury pie crust mix. Stir with a fork until dough holds together. Form into a ball. Sprinkle flour on pastry board or cloth. Rub flour on rolling pin. Roll out to ¼ inch thick and cut into 4-inch squares. Gently lift the squares, one at a time, and place 1 heaping tablespoon filling on one side of the square. Wet the inside edges of the pastry, fold over and press together. Flute the edges with thumb and forefinger. Fry in *hot* oil and butter, turning once, until the pies are *brown* on each side. Serve immediately or make in the morning, place on a cookie sheet lined with aluminum foil and reheat later for 20 minutes in an oven preheated to 325 F. Do not refrigerate after frying.

BEEF AND SAUSAGE FILLING

Cut sausages into ¼-inch slices. Fry sausage, beef, onion, sage, and cloves in Teflon skillet until onion is slightly brown. Add Gravy Master and catsup and stir over low heat for 3 minutes.

HAM FILLING

Chop bacon and fry with ham and onion until onion is slightly browned. Add mustard and cream or milk and stir over medium heat until mixture is moist but not liquidy.

Brown and Crusty Potatoes with Bacon

Whether you're camping out in the north woods or his one-and-a-half-room pad in the Village, these potatoes, plus catsup and fried eggs will provide instant ecstasy.

INGREDIENTS

2 large potatoes, thinly sliced
1 large onion
6 slices bacon
⅛ teaspoon salt
⅛ teaspoon sage (optional)
1 tablespoon cooking oil

DIRECTIONS

Peel, rinse and slice potatoes *thin.* Peel, and slice onion and separate onion rings. Fry bacon slices in a Teflon skillet until they are brown on one side. Turn bacon and arrange neatly in pan. Mix salt and sage with potatoes and onions and arrange neatly over the bacon slices. Fry until potato slices on bottom of pan are crusty and brown. Carefully loosen edges and bottom of potatoes. Place dinner plate over potatoes and turn pan upside down so that potatoes fall neatly onto plate. Heat oil in pan and carefully slide potatoes into pan, with the browned slices on top. Fry for 3 minutes on high then turn flame to low, cover potatoes and cook for 15 to 20 minutes, or until potatoes are soft. Turn flame on high for 2 minutes more. Loosen potatoes and slide them onto a serving plate, bacon slices on top. Serve hot.

Spaghetti with Chicken Livers and Oregano

A great mound of spaghetti topped with chicken livers and

green pepper and sprinkled with oregano—a main course fit for your king, and so easy to prepare!

INGREDIENTS

½ *package thin spaghetti or linguine*
1 *tablespoon salt*
¼ *pound butter*
1 *pound chicken livers, drained*
½ *cup green pepper slices, seeds and pulp removed*
½ *teaspoon dried oregano*
   salt and freshly ground black pepper to taste

DIRECTIONS

Cook spaghetti according to directions on package. Meanwhile, melt butter in skillet. Add green pepper slices and chicken livers. Cook the livers 2 minutes on each side. They should be slightly pink inside but not raw.

Drain spaghetti well. Pour chicken livers, green peppers and butter over drained spaghetti. Sprinkle with oregano and toss. Serve immediately with salt and pepper to taste.

Super-Duper French-Fried Potatoes

Now you can make the best French-fried potatoes in the world! If you're thinking that all French fries taste the same, it's a sure sign *you need this recipe.*

INGREDIENTS

3 *large potatoes* (not *baking potatoes*)
3 *cups cooking oil*
   salt

DIRECTIONS

Peel potatoes and cut into ½″ x ½″ x 3½″ strips. Place potatoes in water to cover and bring to a boil. As soon as the water *begins* to boil, drain the potatoes and place on paper towels for 5 minutes. Meanwhile heat oil in deep-frying pan. Place the *thoroughly** drained potatoes in the boiling oil and fry until golden brown. Drain, sprinkle with salt, and serve immediately.

Jamaican Barbecue Sauce and Hamburgers**

Need an extra-special treat? Want to spend less than ten minutes in the kitchen? Just zap some hamburgers into a pan and stir up this piquant barbecue sauce to serve bubbling hot over those burgers. He'll relish you for it.

INGREDIENTS

1 small green pepper, seeded and chopped
1 small onion, chopped
2 tablespoons butter
½ teaspoon dry musard (or 2 tablespoons mild yellow mustard)
1 tablespoon Worcestershire sauce
1 teaspoon lemon juice
¼ cup catsup
¼ cup brown sugar
½ teaspoon salt
1 pound ground round steak

DIRECTIONS

Melt butter in a pan, add remaining ingredients except ground steak. Stir over medium heat for 5 minutes. Broil or pan fry

All water must be drained from the potatoes or they will cause oil to splatter dangerously.

**This is marvelous cooked in advance and reheated.

hamburgers as you like them. Top with Jamaican Barbecue Sauce served hot or cold.

Sausage Sandwiches

Another man-sized munchable is this Italian treat.

INGREDIENTS

    1 large green pepper
    2 tablespoons cooking oil
    1 large onion
    4 large mushrooms
    ⅛ teaspoon black pepper
    ⅛ teaspoon oregano
    8 Swift's fully cooked Brown 'n' Serve sausages
    ⅓ cup Campbell's bisque of tomato soup, concentrate
        (no water) (cream of tomato may be substituted)
    1 Italian bread

DIRECTIONS

Wash green pepper. Remove pulp, seeds, and stem, cut pepper into ½-inch strips. Place cooking oil in Teflon pan and sauté pepper strips over medium heat for 5 minutes, stirring occasionally. Meanwhile, peel onion into ½-inch slices. Separate slices into rings and stir into pan. Wash, peel, and slice mushrooms and add these to the pepper and onion. Sauté for 3 minutes. Cut sausages lengthwise. Push the vegetables to one side of the pan and turn up the flame. Arrange the sausages cut side down in the pan and fry for 3 minutes. Turn the sausages and spoon the vegetables over them. Fry for 3 minutes more, add the tomato soup concentrate (no water), and stir. Add the pepper and oregano and stir for one minute. Lower flame. Split the bread and cut in half. Remove some of the soft insides of the bread, warm under broiler, heap in the sausages and vegetables. Serve hot.

Creamed-Corn Clam Chowder

A meal in a bowl . . . perfect for cold weather TV watching.

INGREDIENTS

4 slices bacon
1 can Campbell's frozen potato soup
1 package frozen creamed corn
½ cup canned minced clams
½ cup clam juice
½ cup light cream
2 teaspoons butter
paprika

DIRECTIONS

Cut bacon pieces into 1-inch squares and fry over medium heat until cooked but not crisp. Place potato soup and creamed corn in pan. Use a slotted spoon to add ½ cup minced clams to pan. Pour ½ cup clam juice into measuring cup, taking care not to include any sand there may be in the bottom of the can. Add measured clam juice and cream to pan and cook over medium flame until frozen ingredients are thawed and chowder is scalding but not boiling. Ladle soup into soup plates. Top each with 1 teaspoon butter and a dash of paprika. Serve immediately with crusty bread and cold butter.

Special Occasion Spectaculars

Your snacks have been super, your morning-afters a delight, your candlelight dinners divine. Now you feel absolutely confident you are ready to tackle that challenge of challenges… a Special Occasion Spectacular!

The following ten easier-than-pie recipes combine to produce two fantastic meals that will convince his best friends (or even his parents! Gasp! Joy!) that you're a heaven-sent treasure and a wonder in the kitchen.

Menu

CHINESE-Y CHICKEN WINGS
HAM SLICES EN CROUTE
SUPER SPICY PECOT POTATOES
SLICED TOMATOES WITH ANCHOVY DRESSING
TWO-LAYER UPSIDE-DOWN CAKE

Chinese-y Chicken Wings

(Serves 4)

Looking for a tantalizing tidbit that he can nibble with drinks? Save your earlobes for later! Serve him this Chinese-y hors d'oeuvre . . . he'll love it!

INGREDIENTS

20 10 chicken wings
1/2 ¼ cup cooking oil
1/2 4 tablespoons sherry or rum
1/2 4 tablespoons soy sauce
1/2 4 tablespoons honey
1/4 ⅛ teaspoon powdered ginger
1/4 ⅛ teaspoon anise
pinch of cloves

DIRECTIONS

Pull skin from wings. Bring a pot of water to a boil. Drop in chicken wings. When water boils again, remove wings and rinse in cold water. Cut wing into 3 sections, discarding tip. Drain on paper towels. Place oil in Teflon skillet and brown wing sections on both sides. Discard oil. Place remaining ingredients in pan with wing sections and boil over medium heat until sauce is thick and sticks to the wings. Serve warm or cold. (Eat with fingers. These are sticky, so provide lots of napkins.)

Ham Slices en Croute

(Serves 4)

Impressive is the word to describe these ham slices with mushroom stuffing cuddled under a flaky biscuit blanket.

INGREDIENTS

2 ham slices, each ½ inch thick
2 tablespoons butter
5 large fresh mushrooms
1 small onion
½ cup roasted blanched slivered almonds
½ cup bread crumbs
3 tablespoons water
1 egg
1 tablespoon prepared mustard
1 package Pillsbury's quick crescent dinner rolls

MUSTARD SAUCE

1 tablespoon butter
1 tablespoon flour
1 cup milk
¼ teaspoon salt
1½ teaspoons prepared mustard

92

ham steak

DIRECTIONS

Rinse ham slices and pat dry with paper towels. Melt butter in Teflon frying pan. Wash and chop mushrooms (no need to peel if they are very fresh). Peel and chop onion. Sauté mushrooms and onion for 5 minutes, stirring occasionally. Meanwhile, chop the slivered almonds. Remove pan from head and add the almonds, bread crumbs, water, and egg. Stir rapidly until bread crumbs are moistened. Place 1 ham slice on cookie sheet and spread with almond mixture. Top with second ham slice. Spread top with mustard. Bake for 30 minutes in an oven preheated to 350 degrees F. Remove from oven. Cool to room temperature. Twenty minutes before serving time, open package of dinner rolls. Unroll but do not separate. Neatly fit dough over top and sides of the stuffed ham slices. Bake at 375 degrees F. for 20 minutes. Serve immediately with mustard sauce.

MUSTARD SAUCE

Melt butter in pan. Stir in flour. Add milk all at one time. Stir constantly over medium heat until sauce boils. Add mustard and salt. Mix well. Serve hot.

Super Spicy Pecot Potatoes

(Serves 4)

Crispy and unusual. These are potatoes with a difference.

INGREDIENTS

  2 cups grated raw potatoes
  2 eggs
  ¼ teaspoon thyme
  ¼ teaspoon mace
  ¼ teaspoon nutmeg
  ¼ teaspoon salt
  2 tablespoons butter

DIRECTIONS

Peel and grate potatoes. Press off as much of the water as possible. Beat in the eggs and spices. Use 1 tablespoon butter to grease 4 custard cups or 1 glass ovenproof dish (8″ x 8″). Spoon in the potato mixture. Bake for 35 to 40 minutes in an oven preheated to 350 degrees F. After 20 minutes, dot with remaining butter. When potatoes are done, loosen the edges with a knife and turn out onto serving plate. Serve very hot.

Sliced Tomatoes with Anchovy Dressing

(Serves 4)

It's the unexpected *POW!* of anchovy in the dressing that makes the important difference here.

*tomatoes and onions
and anchovies*

INGREDIENTS

    4 large, ripe tomatoes
    1 small Bermuda onion
    2 tablespoons wine vinegar
  ¼ cup olive oil
    2 teaspoons anchovy paste
      freshly ground black pepper to taste

DIRECTIONS

Peel the tomatoes. (If they are very ripe they will peel easily. If not dip each tomato in *scalding* water for a few seconds and then peel.) Cut the tomatoes into fairly thick slices and arrange them on a glass serving plate. Refrigerate. Beat together the vinegar, olive oil and anchovy paste. Peel the onion, cut into thin slices, and separate the rings. Arrange onion on tomato, pour dressing over all, sprinkle with freshly ground black pepper and serve cold.

Two-Layer Pineapple Upside-Down Cake

Not even his mother could bake a lighter, fluffier or more beautiful cake than this one.

INGREDIENTS

    1 box Duncan Hines white deluxe cake mix
1⅓ cups water
    2 egg whites
1½ cups dark brown sugar
    1 1-pound 13½ ounce can Dole sliced pineapple in heavy
      syrup (8 slices)

7 Maraschino cherries

1½ 6½-ounce packages Nestle's butterscotch-flavored Toll
    House morsels

2 tablespoons butter

DIRECTIONS

Preheat oven to 350 degrees F. Blend cake mix, water and egg whites in a large mixing bowl. Beat 2 minutes on high speed and 1 minute on low. Use ½ tablespoon butter each to grease 2 Teflon cake pans. Sprinkle thoroughly with flour. Shake off excess flour. Drain pineapple slices and Maraschino cherries. Sprinkle ¾ cup brown sugar into each pan. Dot with remaining butter.

In one pan arrange pineapple slices as follows: Place 1 whole slice in the center of the pan. Cut 3 slices of the pineapple in half and arrange the half slices around the edges of the pan. Place a cherry in the center ring and tuck the remaining cherries around the outside of the center slice. Carefully smooth one half of the batter over this.

Use a knife and fork to cut the remaining 4 slices of pineapple into small pieces. Sprinkle these over the brown sugar in the second pan. Carefully smooth the remaining batter over this. Bake layers for 30 minutes, then cool them for 5 minutes in the pans. Place a plate upside down over pan (hold it tightly!) and invert. Hold in this position for a few seconds. Repeat process with second layer. Carefully slide layer with cherries onto second layer (fruit side up, naturally).

In a small saucepan, melt the butterscotch bits and the butter. Stir until smooth and spread around the sides of the cake. Serve at room temperature.

Menu

COLD CHICKEN AVOCADO SOUP
ROMAN HONEYED CHICKEN WITH MELON
ENDIVE WITH ORANGE DRESSING
YELLOW RICE
COLD RASPBERRY SOUFFLE

Cold Chicken Avocado Soup

(Serves 4)

Sip this creamy cold soup in champagne glasses. It's the avocado that does the trick.

INGREDIENTS

  1 can cream of chicken soup
  1 ripe avocado
  ⅛ cup lime juice
  4 ice cubes
  2 thin slices lime
  2 thin slices lemon
  paprika

DIRECTIONS

Slice 2 thin slices each lemon and lime. Set aside. Peel avocado. Cut in pieces. Place in blender with cream of chicken soup. Measure ⅛ cup lime juice. Pour into blender. Turn on high speed for 1 minute. Take ice cubes out of tray and place 2 in each bowl. Pour equal amounts of soup in each bowl. Remove ice cubes. Place 1 slice lime and 1 slice lemon carefully on top of each bowl of soup. (Overlap slices for more artistic effect.) Sprinkle with a dash of paprika. Serve immediately.

Roman Honeyed Chicken with Melon

(Serves 4)

Are you a nut for old movies? This recipe is based on the meal served to General Crassius the eve of his battle with Spartacus (from the movie *Spartacus,* naturally). The warm honeyed bird and the icy, succulent melon are an inspired combination.

INGREDIENTS

½ cup Uncle Ben's converted rice
2 boned chicken breasts cut into 1-inch cubes
3 tablespoons butter
⅓ cup honey
3 tablespoons Liquore Galliano (or any anise-flavored liqueur)
1 tablespoon sesame seeds
½ very ripe melon (honeydew or cranshaw is best)

DIRECTIONS

Chill the melon. Cook the rice according to directions on package. Drain the chicken cubes on paper towels. Melt the butter in a Teflon pan. Sauté the chicken for two minutes on each side. Add the honey. Cook for 4 minutes, stirring constantly. Peel the melon, discard the seeds and cut into thin slices. Place a mound of rice on each plate. Reheat the chicken cubes, sprinkle them with sesame seeds and place them on the rice, leaving most of the honey in the pan. Swirl the Liquore Galliano with the remaining honey and pour over the chicken and rice. Arrange cold melon slices around the edges of the plates. Serve immediately.

Endive Salad with Orange Dressing

(Serves 4)

The hint of orange in this salad makes it complement perfectly any meal in which fowl is the main course.

INGREDIENTS

2 tablespoons orange juice
1 tablespoon wine vinegar
½ teaspoon sugar
¼ cup olive oil
4 or 5 fairly large endive stalks
10 pitted black olives, sliced

DIRECTIONS

Beat together orange juice, vinegar, sugar and olive oil. Wash endive stalks and cut them in quarters lengthwise. Drain on paper towels. Slice olives. Arrange endive and sliced olives attractively on serving plate. Shake dressing and pour over salad. Chill for ½ hour. Serve cold.

Yellow Rice

(Serves 4)

Rice is nice nestled under almost anything.

INGREDIENTS

> 6 *strips bacon*
> 1 *onion, chopped*
> 2½ *cups water*
> 1 *teaspoon salt*
> ⅛ *teaspoon saffron*
> ¼ *teaspoon thyme*
> 3 *packets MBT chicken broth mix*
> 1 *cup Uncle Ben's converted rice*

DIRECTIONS

Dice the bacon and place in a 3-quart saucepan. Sauté over low heat while you peel and chop the onion. Stir the bacon, add the onion and sauté until the onion is soft but not brown. Remove the pan from the flame and add the water, salt, saffron, thyme and chicken broth mix. Bring to a boil over high flame. Add the rice, stir, cover and cook over low heat for 25 to 30 minutes or until rice is cooked through but not mushy. Serve hot.

Cold Raspberry Soufflé

(Serves 4 to 6)

A delicate sweet to end an exciting meal is this attractive Raspberry Soufflé.

INGREDIENTS

4 tablespoons raspberry Jell-O
½ cup cold water
2 packages frozen raspberries, thawed
1 cup ripe raspberries or strawberries
⅓ cup Cointreau
2 cups heavy cream
4 tablespoons granulated sugar

DIRECTIONS

In a 3-quart saucepan soften the Jell-O in the cold water and stir over low heat until it is dissolved. Cool to room temperature. Place the thawed raspberries (one package at a time) in the container of your blender. Blend for 1 minute each. Strain the blended berries and stir them into the gelatin. Stir in the Cointreau and chill until the consistency is slightly thicker than that of unbeaten egg white. Watch carefully so the gelatin does not set. Beat the heavy cream until it thickens slightly, sprinkle in the sugar and continue to beat until the cream is stiff. Reserve ¼ cup of the whipped cream and fold the rest into the slightly thickened raspberry-gelatin mixture. Tie a collar of lightly oiled wax paper around the outside of a 1-quart soufflé dish. Spoon in the soufflé and chill until firm. To serve remove the wax paper and garnish with the washed fresh raspberries or strawberries and the reserved whipped cream piped through a fluted nozzle of a pastry bag. Serve very cold.

Love Potions

Aphrodisiac . . . fact or fiction, magic mixture of herbs
and spices or total fantasy?

There are those who believe but can't prove it's
true. And there are those who don't believe but can't
prove it isn't.

Which little witch are you?

Lobster Pernod Flambé

Pernod and absinthe have long been associated with affairs of the heart. According to legend, Parisian artists guzzled it shamelessly to maintain their formidable peak of performance. Here's a more civilized but equally intoxicating way to indulge in its exotic pleasures.

INGREDIENTS

3 small lobsters*
3 cups dry white wine
4 tablespoons butter
1 tablespoon plus one teaspoon flour
¼ teaspoon salt
¼ cup Pernod
1 tablespoon dried tarragon
1½ tablespoons dried chervil
    French bread
2 tablespoons butter

*These are available at your fish store. Ask to have them cleaned and cut, shell and all, into 2-inch pieces and claws cracked. If live lobsters are not sold in your vicinity, substitute 5 lobster tails.

DIRECTIONS

Discard heads of lobsters. Pleace lobster pieces, plus claws, into a broad-based pot or a skillet. Add the wine. Bring to a boil and boil gently, turning the lobster pieces until they are bright red in color. Melt 3 tablespoons butter in a small pan. Stir in flour and salt. Add 1⅓ cup of the cooking wine and stir over medium heat until sauce thickens. Stir in tarragon and chervil. Pick lobster meat from shells and place in a small skillet with 1 tablespoon butter. Heat, add Pernod and set aflame. When flame dies out add lobster and Pernod to sauce. Cut 6 1-inch slices of bread and sauté them in 2 tablespoons melted butter until they are golden brown on each side. Arrange 3 pieces French bread toast on each plate, top with lobster meat and pour sauce over. Decorate each plate with 3 claws. Serve hot.

Sexy Steak Tartare Sandwiches*

I promise that your favorite male will go absolutely wild over raw Steak Tartare. Yes, you heard correctly. Not rare meat but *raw* ground sirloin is the basis for this sexy, man-pleasing snack. Steak tartarte was first proclaimed an aphrodisiac way back in the ninth century, by those virile Tartar tribesmen who were apparently even more skilled out of their saddles than they were *in* them. These savage charmers carried a chunk of raw meat under their saddles to munch on in case they were called upon to debauch a few virgins on short notice. Sex stimulant or merely gourmet non-cooking treat, it's utterly delectable. Better try it!

*Prepare no more than 1 hour in advance of serving or meat will turn dark.

INGREDIENTS

½ pound ground steak.*
1 small sweet onion, finely chopped
4 thin slices dark bread (rye or pumpernickel will do nicely)
1 egg yolk
8 small anchovy slices
8 stuffed olives, sliced
50 capers

DIRECTIONS

Peel and chop onion. Drain the anchovy fillets on paper toweling. Lightly mix the egg yolk and chopped onion with the meat. Spread this on the bread slices. Criss-cross with anchovy fillets. Decorate the meat with capers and olive slices. Refrigerate.

Bloody Mary with a Difference

A Bloody Mary traditionally is a vodka and tomato juice pick-me-up. The difference in this terrific potion? A raw clam or oyster slipped into the bottom of every glass. If the vodka doesn't inspire you, the seafood surely will.

INGREDIENTS

(for each Bloody Mary)

1½ ounces vodka
⅓ cup tomato juice

---

*Packaged chopped meat *will not do!* Make sure the meat is *super* fresh by purchasing as close to serving time as possible. Also ask the butcher to trim away the fat and put the meat through a grinder that has not been used for grinding pork.

1 teaspoon lemon juice

¼ teaspoon Worcestershir sauce

½ teaspoon granulated sugar

3 drops Tabasco sauce

2 ice cubes

salt and pepper

1 raw clam or oyster, freshly opened

DIRECTIONS

Mix together the vodka, tomato juice, lemon juice, Worcestershire sauce, sugar, Tabasco sauce and ice cubes. Pour the drink into a glass without the ice cubes. Slip the clam or oyster along with its juice into the glass. Sprinkle with salt and pepper and serve immediately.

Marrakech Meatballs

(Serves 4)

Intriguing Marrakech in Morocco sends this sweet and spicy recipe our way. According to our culinary spies in the East, these exotic spices blend with the honey and fruit to produce a subtle aphrodisiac effect. Is it truly the spices that enhance love or the hashish the natives are rumored to include? I'm not in a position to say. I tested the recipe . . . but without the forbidden drug. All I can attest to is the sublime taste. Serves four . . . invite a friendly couple.

INGREDIENTS

MEAT BALLS

1½ pounds beef neck, ground
1 slice bread
3 tablespoons milk
1 tablespoon raisins
¼ teaspoon thyme
¼ teaspoon allspice
¼ teaspoon salt
2 tablespoons cooking oil

SAUCE

14 pitted prunes
10 dried apricots
3 tablespoons honey
1 can Campbell's beef consommé
½ can water
1 tablespoon soy sauce
½ teaspoon allspice
1 teaspoon cinnamon
rice or Minute Rice

DIRECTIONS

MEAT BALLS

Soak bread in milk. Mash into a paste. Add ground meat, raisins, thyme, allspice and salt. Mix well and form into meatballs approximately 1 inch in diameter. Pour cooking oil into Teflon skillet. Brown meatballs on all sides. Do not overcook.

SAUCE

Pour meatballs and any liquid in pan into an ovenproof dish with a cover. Tuck the prunes and apricots among the meatballs.

Add the honey, consommé, water, soy sauce, allspice and cinnamon. Cover and bake for 1 hour at 325 degrees F. Meanwhile cook rice according to directions on package. Serve meatballs and sauce on a bed of rice.

Blanched Almond Soup*

Ground almonds and spices—a combination to remember.

INGREDIENTS

½ can cream of celery soup
½ can cream of chicken soup
¾ cup blanched almonds
   one pinch each: mace, thyme, nutmeg, dry mustard,
   rosemary
½ cup milk
¾ cup heavy cream

DIRECTIONS

Place ½ can each cream of celery soup, cream of chicken soup, and heavy cream into sauce pan. Stir. Place over low heat. Meanwhile, put blanched almonds through grinder or chop in blender. Add spices and soup to blender. Blend on high speed for 30 seconds—*no longer.* Reheat if necessary. Serve hot. Sprinkle with a few grains each of mace, nutmeg, and paprika. Top with a few blanched almonds arranged around a tiny sprig of parsley set in the middle of each bowl.

*May be prepared several hours in advance and reheated without boiling when ready to serve. Garnish immediately before serving.

Curried Shrimp with Apple

Eve had a way with apples. Follow this recipe and you will have, too.

INGREDIENTS

24 frozen shrimp, medium to large size
1 apple, medium size
1 onion, small
2 tablespoons butter
2 tablespoons flour
1 tablespoon curry powder
¼ teaspoon salt
1½ cup milk
1 packet MBT chicken broth mix
1 cup rice
2 tablespoons slivered almonds
2 tablespoons raisins

DIRECTIONS

Prepare shrimp according to directions on package. Peel, core, and slice apple. Melt butter in skillet. Sauté apple and onion for ten minutes over fairly low flame. *Do not allow to brown.* Sprinkle flour, curry powder and salt over apple and onion. Mix thoroughly. Add milk all at one time and stir until sauce thickens, mashing out any lumps with the back of the spoon. Add chicken broth mix and simmer for five minutes. Prepare rice according to directions on package. Heap rice on plate, top with curry, garnish with almonds and raisins. Serve hot.

Spaghetti with Oyster Sauce

OYSTERS! Are they merely delicious shellfish or are their legendary reputations well deserved? The perfect meal to cook at his place. (If garlic doesn't excite you, substitute one tablespoon dried minced onion.)

INGREDIENTS

½ package thin spaghetti or linguine
1 tablespoon salt
¼ pound butter
3 tablespoons olive oil
1 clove garlic, crushed, or ¼ teaspoon garlic powder
2 tablespoons dried parsley flakes
¼ teaspoon Tabasco sauce
1 8-ounce can frozen oysters
1 tablespoon chopped chives

DIRECTIONS

Cook spaghetti according to directions on package. Meanwhile melt butter in skillet. Add olive oil, crushed garlic or garlic

chives

powder, parsley flakes and Tabasco sauce. Chop the oysters reserving their juices. Spoon the minced oysters with their juice into the pan. (Leave several spoonfuls of juice in the bottom of the can. *Do not pour* oysters into pan just in case there should be a few gritty pieces in the bottom of the can.) Cook until mixture begins to bubble. Drain the spaghetti thoroughly and toss with the oyster sauce. Serve immediately in large shallow bowls. Sprinkle with chopped chives.

Rum Cow

Tastes like the most sublime milk shake ever . . . but watch it! It packs a tremendous wallop, especially when accompanied by a full moon.

INGREDIENTS

1½ cups cold milk
1 scoop vanilla ice cream
1 banana
3 tablespoons sugar
2 ice cubes
⅓ cup rum
¼ cup Pernod

DIRECTIONS

Blend milk, ice cream, banana, sugar and ice on high speed for 30 seconds. Add rum and Pernod and blend on low speed for 10 seconds. Serve immediately or sooner!

Ice Cream of Curry Soup*

Spice up your life with curry soup. Pale golden, cold, and oh, so delicious, this summertime favorite will win plaudits in winter time too! But don't take my word for it. Try it and see!

INGREDIENTS

    1 can cream of chicken soup
    ½ cup heavy cream
    1 teaspoon curry powder
    1 egg yolk
    2 ice cubes

DIRECTIONS

Open can and place cream of chicken soup in blender with ½ cup heavy cream, 1 teaspoon curry powder and 1 egg yolk. Blend for 1 minute on high speed. Pour equal amounts into serving bowls. Place one ice cube in each bowl. Serve very cold.

Red Caviar on Toast Points

Have an aphrodisiac for breakfast and see what surprises the day may have in store! For some strange reason caviar has, through the centuries, been proclaimed a restorer of sexual vitality. If you or your love need any revitalizing, try this! The very worst that can happen is that you'll have consumed a delicious snack.

*May be prepared several hours before serving. Refrigerate until needed. Stir or blend for 5 seconds before pouring into bowls. Garnish immediatly before serving. This dish is beautiful served in silver bowls and topped with paprika. The ice cubes are especially nice if they have been frozen with a small slice of lime and a shrimp in each one.

INGREDIENTS

112

1 4-ounce jar red caviar
4 slices white bread
1 tablespoon butter
1 tablespoon cream cheese
6 black olives, pitted
2 wedges lemon

DIRECTIONS

Drain caviar in a strainer. Toast bread. While hot, spread 2 slices with butter and two with cream cheese. Slice the olives into "rings." Place the caviar in the center of an attractive plate. Cut the toast into quarters and arrange it neatly around the caviar. Decorate the caviar with olive slices and lemon wedge. Enjoy.

lemon wedge

Marvelous Somethings
Like Mother Used to Make

Have you tried everything you could think of and failed to impress him? Has he scoffed at your Caviar Omelette and cast aspersions on your Cheese Fondue? Make him feel secure with these homespun favorites "like mother used to make." Bread, chocolate chip cookies, apple pie . . . if he isn't kneeling at your feet with a wedding ring after he nibbles these goodies, forget him! He'd be impossible to live with anyway.

Apple Pie

Apple pie served hot with ice cream. Heavenly! Apple pie the old-fashioned way, served cold with milk and sugar. Yum! However you serve it, this recipe will make you the apple of his eye.

INGREDIENTS

CRUST

2 boxes *Pillsbury pie crust mix*
8 tablespoons cold water
2½ tablespoons butter

FILLING

6 *extra-large pippin apples*
¾ *cup granulated sugar*
1 *teaspoon ground nutmeg*
1 *teaspoon cinnamon*
⅛ *teaspoon mace*
1 *tablespoon lemon juice*
3 *tablespoons granulated sugar*
3 *tablespoons butter*

DIRECTIONS

CRUST

Mix butter with water and add to pie crust mix. Continue according to directions on package. This pie filling is very bulky and requires slightly more crust that one package makes. Use any remaining dough to make Fried Meat Pies.

FILLING

Peel and core apples and cut them into eights. Mix the apples, ¾ cup sugar and spices and cook in a saucepan over a low flame for 5 minutes. Cool to room temperature. Spoon the filling into the unbaked pie shell. Sprinkle with lemon juice and the remaining sugar. Dot with butter. Roll out the top crust and fit it over the pie. Crimp the edges. Cut some ½ inch slits in the top and bake for 15 minutes in an oven preheated to 450 degrees F. Reduce the oven heat to 375 degrees F. and bake for 30 minutes more. Remove the pie from the oven, but do not turn oven off. Brush the top (not the edges) of the pie with cream, sprinkle with a little sugar, return to the oven and bake for 10 minutes more. Remove pie from the oven. Serve warm or cold.

Poppy Seed Bread

(Serves umpteen—so have a party)

For that small town fella alone in the city, for the mamma's boy who just won't let go, for the sophistocate who's really a little boy at heart, or even for your friend Georgie who once lived next-door to a bakery . . . home-baked bread is the unbeatable eatable.

INGREDIENTS

> 2 envelopes yeast*
> ¼ cup lukewarm water
> ¾ cup milk
> ¼ cup cream
> 8 tablespoons butter
> 1 tablespoon granulaed sugar
> 1 teaspoon salt
> 4 cups all-purpose flour measured after sifting
> 2 eggs, beaten
> ¼ cup dried minced onion
> ⅓ cup poppy seeds

*Check back of envelope to make sure it isn't outdated.

DIRECTIONS

Place the lukewarm water in a fairly large, flat bowl and sprinkle the yeast over it. Scald the milk and the cream and place in a large mixing bowl with 5 tablespoons butter (reserve the rest for later use), sugar and ½ teaspoon salt. Cool this to lukewarm and stir in 2 cups sifted flour. This will produce a sticky batter, not a dough. Stir the yeast and when it has softened completely, stir it alternately with the beaten eggs into the sticky batter. Beat this thoroughly. Sift the remainder of the flour with ½ teaspoon salt and stir enough of this into the batter to produce a soft dough. If the dough is too sticky to handle, add flour until it can be handled without its sticking to the fingers. Turn out the dough onto a lightly floured board or the scrubbed formica top of a cabinet. Knead by folding one edge of the dough inward and pressing it down firmly with the knuckles. Turn the dough and repeat this process over and over, until the dough is smooth and has a satiny sheen. (This should take about 15 minutes of vigorous kneading.)

Place the dough in a large buttered bowl, cover with a clean dish towel and let it rise for 2 hours in a place that is warm and free from drafts. (If your oven has a pilot light, place the dough in the oven and close the door. *Do not light the oven.)*

When the dough has doubled in bulk, roll it into a rectangle ½ inch thick. Brush this with 3 tablespoons softened butter and sprinkle with the minced onion and the poppy seeds. Roll like a jelly roll and bend the rolled dough around into a ring, pinching the ends together with thumb and forefinger. Brush the ring with butter and sprinkle lightly with poppy seeds. Place on a buttered baking sheet and cut it from the top to within ½ inch from the bottom in slices at 1-inch intervals around the ring. Bend each slice slightly to the side. The result will be an attractive ring with "pinwheels" of dough bent to reveal swirls of poppy seed filling. Cover with a dish towel and once again let the ring rise in a warm, draft-free place, until it has doubled in bulk. Bake for 25 to 30 minutes in an oven preheated to 350 degrees F. Serve warm or cooled, with mounds of butter.

All-American Meat Loaf

(Serves 4 or serves 2, with meat loaf sandwiches for tomorrow)

What has catsup and mustard and hamburger and a crumpled up roll? All-American Meat Loaf, of course.

INGREDIENTS

2 pounds ground round steak
¼ cup celery, chopped
1 medium onion, chopped
1 tablespoon cooking oil
1 hamburger roll (or 1½ slices white bread)
¼ cup milk
⅓ teaspoon salt
⅛ teaspoon pepper
¼ teaspoon sage
¼ teaspoon thyme
4 tablespoons catsup
2 tablespoons mild yellow mustard

DIRECTIONS

Place meat in large mixing bowl. Sauté chopped celery and onion in cooking oil until soft but not brown. Crumble hamburger roll (or bread) in a small bowl, add the milk and stir.

Squeeze excess milk from the bread. Add the bread, the sautéed celery and onion, the spices, the catsup and the mustard to the meat. Use your fingers to quickly and gently mix the ingredients. *Do not overmix.* Place in a loaf pan, smooth top and decorate with alternate stripes of catsup and mustard. Bake for 1 hour in an oven preheated to 350 degrees F. Pour off excess grease. Serve hot.

County Fair Potato Salad*

This is not the ordinary variety of slippery, pallid potato salad. No M'am! This is the chunky, pungent, homespun kind you find taking prizes at county fairs. Serve him this . . . maybe you'll take home a prize!

INGREDIENTS

14 very small or new potatoes
4 eggs, hard-cooked
¾ cup mayonnaise
2 tablespoons mild yellow mustard
½ teaspoon salt
¼ cup sweet pickle, chopped
2 tablespoons pickle juice
⅓ cup celery, chopped
¼ cup onion, chopped
½ teaspoon poppy seeds
10 pimento-stuffed olives, sliced
4 sweet pickles cut in strips
paprika

*Potato salad actually tastes better the day after it's made. Why not prepare it one or even two days in advance of serving? Just be sure to keep it covered and well chilled.

DIRECTIONS

Boil the whole potatoes in their skins until they are cooked through but not mushy. Hard-cook the eggs. Peel the cooled potatoes, removing all of the black specks. Peel the hard-cooked eggs. Chop the potatoes and 3½ eggs into ½-inch cubes. Mix the mayonnaise, mustard, salt, chopped pickle, pickle juice, chopped celery, chopped onion and poppy seeds and add to the potatoes and eggs. Mix well. Spoon potato salad into a glass serving bowl. Decorate the top with reserved ½ hard-cooked egg (yolk side up), strips of pickle and slices of olive. Dust the outside edges with paprika. Chill thoroughly. Serve cold.

Baked Stuffed Potatoes

What goes best with just plain steak? Baked Stuffed Potatoes. of course.

INGREDIENTS

2 medium size baking potatoes
4 slices bacon
1 small onion
2½ tablespoons milk
2 tablespoons butter
salt and pepper to taste

DIRECTIONS

Wash and dry potatoes. Rub skins with a little cooking oil or butter. Bake at 400 degrees F. for 1 hour. (If potatoes are larger than average, they may take a bit longer.)

Meanwhile dice bacon fine. Peel onion and chop fine. Sauté

bacon and onion until onion is golden but not browned. Pour off all but one tablespoon bacon grease. Cut potatoes in half, lengthwise. Scoop out centers and whip with the milk and one tablespoon butter. Add bacon, one tablespoon drippings, onion, salt and pepper and whip again. Heap potatoes high in one half of each shell, dot tops with butter. Place on a baking sheet and bake for 10 minutes in an oven preheated to 500 degrees F. Serve at once.

Cole Slaw*

Cole slaw is picnic-type food, so if your man is the picnic type . . . serve this.

INGREDIENTS

½ small head cabbage
1 cup mayonnaise
⅓ cup milk
3 tablespoons lemon juice
3 tablespoons granulated sugar
¾ teaspoon salt
1 teaspoon poppy seeds
3 tablespoons crushed pineapple without juice (optional)

DIRECTIONS

Cut the half cabbage into four wedges. Cut out and discard hard core. Wash and drain quarters. Use a large chopping knife to cut cabbage into fine shreds. Chop the shreds into ½ inch pieces. Place in a large glass bowl. In a separate bowl mix mayonnaise, milk, lemon juice, sugar, salt, poppy seeds and crushed

*Cole slaw keeps for several days and actually improves with age. Therefore this recipe is enough to feed four . . . or two and two.

pineapple. Pour this over the chopped cabbage and mix well. Wipe inside of bowl with a paper towel. Refrigerate cole slaw until serving time.

Sweet Baking Powder Biscuits for Your Sweet

(Makes 6 biscuits)

The girl who can make great baking powder biscuits can do anything! And these biscuits *are* great!

INGREDIENTS

>   1 cup all-purpose flour
>   2 tablespoons granulated sugar
> ¼ teaspoon salt
>   2 teaspoons baking powder
>   3 tablespoons butter
>   2 tablespoons milk
>   1 egg
>   Butter and jam as desired

DIRECTIONS

Sift together the first four ingredients. Use a pastry cutter or two knives to cut in 3 tablespoons butter to produce a mealy mixture. Beat the egg and the milk together and stir this into the sifted dry ingredients to form a soft dough. Turn the dough onto a floured surface and pat into a circle about 6 inches in diameter, turning once. Use the mouth of a small glass to cut out 6 biscuits. Grease a baking pan, place the biscuits on it and bake for 15 minutes in an oven preheated to 400 degrees F., or until golden brown. Split biscuits while hot and butter. Serve with preserves or jam.

Plain, Simple, Delicious Beef Stew
(Serves 4)

Not much of a cook? Stop fretting—*start* stewing! Be he American, French, Italian, or Israeli, no man can resist stew-pendous you!

INGREDIENTS

    2 pounds round steak
1½ tablespoons cooking oil
    2 medium size onions
    2 medium size carrots
    2 cups water
 ½ cup tomato juice
    4 packets MBT beef broth mix
    1 teaspoon Gravy Master
 ¼ teaspoon thyme
 ½ teaspoon sage
 ⅛ teaspoon pepper
 ½ teaspoon salt
    1 large bay leaf
    4 medium size potatoes
 16 large mushrooms
    1 tablespoon cornstarch
    2 tablespoons water

DIRECTIONS

Cut steak into 2-inch pieces, discarding fat. Heat oil in a large heavy pan with a lid. Brown meat on all sides. Peel onions and cut into quarters. Peel carrots and cut into ½ inch slices. Add onions, carrots, water, tomato juice, beef broth mix, Gravy Master and spices to pan. Stir. Cover and cook over very low flame for 1 hour and 15 minutes. Meanwhile, peel potatoes and cut into quarters. Wash mushrooms, trim stems and cut in half. (If mushrooms are very fresh, there is no need to peel them.) Add potatoes and mushrooms and cook for 45 minutes more or until potatoes are cooked through. Mix cornstarch and water and stir into a paste. Add to pan and stir constantly over high flame until stew thickens. Serve immediately or refrigerate and reheat at serving time.

Home Baked Beans*

These baked beans begin with the canned variety and end being baked by you for maximum flavor. If you don't give away the secret of their humble beginnings they certainly won't.

INGREDIENTS

½ 14-ounce can butter beans
1 8-ounce can baked beans
4 slices bacon
½ green pepper
½ onion
¼ cup molasses
¼ cup catsup
2 tablespoons mild yellow mustard
4 whole cloves
2 small bay leaves

*These keep very well, so if you're pressed for time better prepare them a day or two in advance. Just cook and refrigerate but do not bake until ready to serve.

DIRECTIONS

Drain butter beans. Cut bacon strips in half and fry over medium heat for 4 minutes, turning once. Remove stem, pulp, and seeds from ½ green pepper and cut into strips. Peel and slice ½ onion. Sauté the green pepper and onion with the bacon for 4 minutes more. Add the baked beans, drained butter beans, molasses, catsup, mustard, cloves and bay leaves to the pan. Stir over medium heat for 2 or 3 minutes. Pour into an earthenware dish, small bean pot or ovenproof glass bowl. Bake for 20 minutes in an oven preheated to 350 degrees F.

Coconut Chewies

No man who was ever a little boy can resist a sexy chick who can also bake cookies!

INGREDIENTS

½ cup Crisco
1 cup brown sugar, tightly packed
1 egg
¾ cup flour, sifted
¼ teaspoon baking soda
⅛ teaspoon baking powder
¼ teaspoon salt
¼ teaspoon cinnamon
½ cup coconut, grated
1¼ cups rolled oats, uncooked
¼ cut walnut halves broken into quarters
¼ cup raisins
¾ cup semi-sweet chocolate chips

DIRECTIONS

Cream together shortening and sugar. Add egg and mix well. Sift together the flour, baking soda, baking powder, salt and cinnamon. Add to creamed mixture and mix until well blended. Add coconut, oats, nuts, raisins, and chocolate chips. Stir. Drop a teaspoonful at a time on an ungreased cookie sheet. Bake at 350 degrees F. for 10 to 12 minutes.

Strawberry Shortcake Like Grandma Used to Make

Even though you wear all the latest fashions are you really an old-fashioned girl at heart? No? It doesn't matter . . . you both will still love the sublime flavor of this old-fashioned strawberry shortcake.

INGREDIENTS

1 cup all-purpose flour
2 tablespoons granulated sugar
¼ teaspoon salt
2 teaspoons baking powder
3 tablespoons butter
2 tablespoons milk
1 egg
2 tablespoons butter
1 quart strawberries
6 tablespoons granulated sugar
¾ cup heavy cream
1 tablespoon granulated sugar
½ teaspoon vanilla

strawberry shortcake

DIRECTIONS

Preheat oven to 375 degrees F. Sift together the first four ingredients. Use a pastry cutter or two knives to cut in 3 tablespoons butter to produce a mealy mixture. Beat the egg and the milk together and stir this into the sifted dry ingredients to form a soft dough. Turn the dough onto a floured surface and pat into a thick circle about 4 inches in diameter turning once. Grease a 4- or 5-inch skillet and press the dough to fit. Bake at 375 degrees F. for 15 to 20 minutes or until golden brown.

Place the hot shortcake on a wire rack to cool slightly. Split the shortcake into two layers and butter the inside surfaces. Wash the strawberries and remove the stems. Slice ½ the strawberries and sprinkle them with 6 tablespoons sugar. Chill. Whip the cream with 1 tablespoon sugar and the vanilla. Chill.

Place the bottom layer of shortcake on a serving plate and cover with the sliced strawberries and half of the whipped cream. Top with the other half of the shortcake. Spread with the remaining whipped cream and decorate with the whole berrics. Serve at once.